Ag

The Church in China

Against All Odds:

THE CHURCH IN CHINA

CARL LAWRENCE

Marshall-Pickering

Marshall Morgan and Scott
Marshall Pickering
3 Beggarwood Lane, Basingstoke, Hants RG23 7LP, UK

First published in the USA in 1985 by
Bethany House Publishers
First UK edition published in 1986 by Marshall Morgan and Scott
Publications Ltd
Part of the Marshall Pickering Holdings Group
A subsidiary of the Zondervan Corporation

British Library CIP Data

Lawrence, Carl
The Church in China: how it survives and prospers under Communism.
1. Christianity—China
I. Title
275.1'0828 BR1285
ISBN 0-551-01243-9

Reproduced, printed and bound in Great Britain by
Hazell Watson & Viney Limited,
Member of the BPCC Group,
Aylesbury, Bucks

The Author

CARL LAWRENCE, Program Director for the Haven of Rest radio broadcast, was for almost 20 years a missionary in Southeast Asia and Director of Programming for the Far East Broadcasting Company. He is married, the father of two, and they make their home in southern California.

Special Acknowledgment

Very little, if any, of this book would have been possible without the complete cooperation, and trust, of a very special group of people. I refer to those who daily give time and energy in the often unnoticed, and equally as often unrecognized, ministry of China research.

Their labors give substance and life to the understanding of the working of the Body of Christ in the People's Republic of China.

To Dr. Jonathan Chao and his staff of the Chinese Church Research Center, Hong Kong; Dr. Theodore Shueh and his staff of the Christian Communications Center, Ltd., Hong Kong; Dr. David Wang of Asian Outreach; Mr. Ken Lo and his staff of F.E.B.C. Associates, Hong Kong; and of course Brothers David, Pablo and Todd of Open Doors, all of whom supplied so much of the information and logistics; acknowledgment is gratefully given, and this book is respectfully dedicated.

[illegible]

Special Acknowledgment

[illegible]

Foreword

This moving story is an epochal book. It marks the end of one age and the beginning of another. It tells of a dramatic new power available for world evangelization.

Until the past twenty years, the spread of the Christian faith was done primarily by the spoken word. As Christians have witnessed to their faith by word and deed, proclaimed Christ, preached the Good News, and persuaded men and women to become Christ's disciples and responsible members of His church, congregations have multiplied in country after country.

This process has been speeded up by a second means, the written/printed word. As men have read portions of the Bible, tracts, and other Christian literature, they have become followers of Jesus Christ our Lord.

During the past twenty years, however, in China these two means of spreading the gospel have been greatly assisted by radio broadcasts. Christians outside China have beamed many hours of the Good News in all its various forms into China through Haven of Rest, Far East Broadcasting Company, TransWorld Radio, and many other missionary radio companies.

A new epoch in world evangelism had dawned. To be sure, many questioned whether it would be effective. By itself it might not have been. But since there were in China four or five million Christians, and several hundred thousand of these were ardent believing Christians, and since the Word of God could be copied by hand and circulated, radio began greatly to extend the effectiveness of the primary and secondary method. Furthermore, as new believers and new bands of believers arose, they spoke to an ever-expanding number of friends. These also listened in secret, and some of them, too, became ardent believers.

The process was helped by the fact that Chairman Mao's Great Leap Forward turned out to be a great leap backward, and millions of Chinese came to the bitter conclusion that communism was bankrupt. It was not delivering what it promised. It could not be the truth. Standing in this vacuum, the listeners heard the gospel over the air with receptive minds.

Readers of this book may sometimes wonder where Carl Lawrence got the detailed information, the facts, and the personal experiences which have made this such a convincing volume. The answer is simple. During the past five years, tens of thousands of Chinese living outside mainland China have been permitted to go back, visit their relatives and see the villages and countryside in which they were born. These visitors talking to their families *when no one was listening* have heard surprising accounts. They have been amazed at the spread of the Christian faith. They have talked to old Christians and to many new Christians. They have found groups of believers where none existed before. They have found that sometimes a tenth of a commune, sometimes a third, sometimes a half, and occasionally a whole commune have become Christian. Groups of believers, some small and some large, were meeting in homes, in gardens, in cemeteries, in forests and fields to study God's Word and worship the Lord.

Furthermore, a few men and women, including the author, have been sent to China to travel widely, supposedly to gather information about the general state of affairs. These have with great discretion sought out house church leaders and have made inquiries on a rather large scale. They have reported many of the facts, incidents, and case histories which Carl Lawrence reports.

Many other evidences make me believe that this volume is credible. A remarkable growth of the church in China has been and is occurring. How big it is no one can say. Some responsible researchers say that there are 20 million adherents of house churches in China. Some say 50 million, some say 75 million, and some say 100 million. While the exact number is impossible to determine, there can be no doubt that a very large number of Christians now exist.

To be sure, few of these followers of the Christ and believers in the Bible would fit exactly any of the denominational patterns in North America. They are certainly not Lutherans, Roman Catholics, Wesleyans, or Presbyterians. But *they are Christians*. These groups of believers are a praying, believing, witnessing church.

Read this epochal book with rejoicing. Praise God for the great victories won in mainland China. Indeed, God has been doing a mighty work in our great sister nation China. And press forward with world evangelization with new hope in your hearts.

Donald McGavran
Dean Emeritus
School of Church Growth
Fuller Theological Seminary

Contents

Introduction

This book had its genesis in 1968. I had just moved to Hong Kong to help establish a Communications Research Center, with special emphasis on the People's Republic of China.

You may recall that 1968 was a very difficult time for China. The Cultural Revolution had spilled over into Hong Kong itself. It was not uncommon on the way to work to walk around an unexploded bomb with a Communist flag attached. Every evening the financial section of the city was the site of another "spontaneous" pro-Mao demonstration.

But what was happening in Hong Kong was not even an infinitesimal hint of the anarchy taking place inside China itself.

The Red Guard was on the rampage.[1]

People were killing and being killed.

Families were being torn apart, as fathers and mothers were being sent to "reeducation" camps.

Schools were closed, along with most businesses and factories.

The borders were sealed and information was at a premium.

[1]Teenage students that were organized by Mao in and out of the People's Liberation Army and first appeared in mid-1966 wearing arm bands imprinted with words "Hong Wei Bing" (Red Guards) and carrying copies of the "little red book"—quotations from Chairman Mao. Acting under the leadership of Mao, they were the vanguards, judge, jury and executioners of the Cultural Revolution.

Information which was garnered from those who swam out, or escaped by other means, was not only strikingly abhorrent to civilized people, but served as a pathetic verification of the worst which one could imagine a leadership doing to its people.

Every radio station in China was playing martial music, or broadcasting the sound of thousands of voices shouting praises to Mao. "The east wind is prevailing over the west wind, and it is we that shall win, for history is on our side," came from millions of screaming, frenzied youth, who held up their "little red book" which matched the red arm band, marking them as members of the Red Guard.

All music from the West—Mozart to Mantovani—was banned, along with Western literature and other art forms. Anyone who had in his possession such materials was "counter-revolutionary" and had to be purged from the party through public "self-confession" meetings, followed by a sentence which could be prison or death.

Mao and his Red Guards were purifying the revolution. The slogan "Long live Chairman Mao" replaced all rational thinking.

Now, a decade and a half later, Mao is dead. His revolution, his "little red book," and the Red Guard are all in disgrace. Like Mao's body, they rot away as relics to be swept into history's dust bin.

Instead of martial music, you might hear a smuggled cassette tape of Dolly Parton singing the patently capitalistic song "Nine to Five."

Not only are Mozart and Beethoven back, but so is Henry Mancini plus many of the present Western "pop" artists.

People no longer have to crawl under a blanket in order to listen to foreign Christian radio. Researchers in Hong Kong not only don't have to wait seven years for a response to their programs, but can actually travel into China for personal interviews.

The dull blue Mao jackets are gradually being replaced, at least in the major cities, by some colorful prints.

Military operas have given way to violins, guitars and orchestras that sound very much like Lawrence Welk, playing excerpts from "The Sound of Music."

A rather sultry rendition of "Yankee Doodle Dandy," done by an equally sultry Chinese maiden, dressed in a sequined evening gown, may draw the largest applause of the evening at regularly scheduled pop concerts. This is more meaningful when you realize that it is the theme song for Voice of America which continues to broadcast to China.

The boards are slowly coming off the stained-glass windows. Grain and other storage items are being sent to less colorful warehouses, as some of the churches are being officially "re-opened." Bibles, like all illegal counterrevolutionary materials which were carefully wrapped in oiled paper and buried, are being dug up.

The people are beginning to talk, to smile, and even in some cases to laugh out loud in the presence of a "foreigner."

Slowly, in deliberate, measured tones and long periods of embarrassed silence, the people are beginning to tell the story of what really happened during the "great purge" known almost romantically in the West, but not in China, as the "Cultural Revolution."

As they speak, the words keep attacking one's senses: "No," we want to tell ourselves as we set the testimonies aside, "this could not have happened. It is an impossibility in this day of human rights, instant communications, press coverage and super-intelligence." The sad and inescapable fact is, it did.

This book is an attempt to share a few of the years of suffering, pain and finally victory.

At this point it is important that we keep several things in mind as we read this book.

1. "Where did this information come from? Is it accurate?" This very problem created no small amount of dissonance in my own mind. While writing in a hotel room in Hong Kong, I was tempted more than once to write a "historical novel." However, I began to realize that many of the actual events seem unbelievable, a figment of someone's imagination and would be considered so in a novel.

Therefore, I settled for a rather simple story broken into two parts: their testimonies and my observations. I hope that I, for the most part, avoided the temptation to editorialize, but at the same time realize that "objectivity" is, at best, a difficult goal. I have settled for presenting testimonies with minimum comment, while still being faithful to a dual commitment: to keep faith with those in China who (1) wanted this book written; (2) wanted their anonymity preserved. Some were even against using false names, dates and places, just in case a similar event might have happened to a person whose name I used in a fictitious way.

Much of the information reported is still very sensitive. The Chinese are acutely and painfully aware that the impossible often happens in China—not once, or even twice, but many times. For that reason it is necessary not to use any real names except when they are well-known persons. Also, cities, counties, etc., are simply referred to in broad geographic terms. One cannot go into great detail about the physical structure of either locations or people in case they might be identified. Every attempt is made not to jeopardize those who were willing to share this information.

To us who live in a free society, this may not seem like much of a problem. For those who have lost their families, their vocation, and in many cases their physical freedom, this is no small consideration. We must look at it from their context.

Still fresh in the minds of many Chinese are two major campaigns: "Let a hundred flowers bloom, let a hundred schools of thought contend," and the "Cultural Revolution."

The first came in mid-1956. After seven years of severe mental suppression, there was an official liberalization to "speak one's mind." This was especially true for the intelligentsia. The unexpected happened. There was a "whirlwind" of criticism of nearly all aspects of the system, the party and its leadership. By mid-1957, those who "spoke their mind," either publicly or in writing, were arrested. Thousands of people were imprisoned. The intelligentsia was decimated. Whether the "Let a hundred flowers bloom" was a devise to ferret out the "rightists" or triggered a fear of "liberalization" in the leadership made little difference. Never again would men and women trust the leadership. Even today, most information, which is not secret by most standards, is exchanged in walks in parks or other public venues. They have learned their lesson well.

The second "washing of the minds" came ten years later in the Cultural Revolution. Its results, as you will find in this book, were even more disastrous to the people of China, and again, especially for the intelligentsia.

Comprehending this, one might better understand why it is necessary to avoid information that can pinpoint events to people, places and time. I am well aware of the decrease of credibility that this creates. I am equally aware of a commitment made in good faith, and without hesitation will opt for complete preservation of the original commitment of confidentiality.[2]

2. Some of the testimonies may seem to be more American than Chinese. Keep in mind that these are literal translations, edited for the Western mind.

3. Some of the stories contain considerable detailed information. How could one remember them in such detail?

—The Chinese education system emphasizes memorization.
—The Chinese language lends itself well to note-taking.
—We all tend to remember the details of the most significant event of our lives.
—There were some people in China who felt it was their mission to tell this story to the world. The Chinese do not have copies of printed sermons or cassettes available in the foyer. For this reason, they listen much more intently and many take notes. This is proving to be a superb source for those in China who are working on a highly technical textbook on this church.

It is not the desire of the Chinese to expose the cruelty of a regime as much as to tell of the love of Jesus Christ. They are not telling their story to get even with those who persecuted them, but to testify to the love and power of the One who saved them.

4. This book is not anti-Chinese. Alexander Solzhenitsyn pointed out in one of his books, "Mother Russia is not the same

[2]Most of the testimonies are available in original language and are available to the serious scholar. The final manuscript has been approved by sources in China and Hong Kong.

as the USSR." This is true of China. Almost to a person, the Chinese are affectionate, tender, loving people. Unfortunately, like their counterparts in Russia, they are controlled by a small minority of cruel, selfish men known as the leadership of the Communist Party. It is not the average Chinese who would execute a young person and then demand the parents reimburse them for the bullets. When we speak of China, sometimes we are talking about the officials in Beijing (formerly called Peking), and other times about those 950 million "others" disenfranchised by a Marxist regime.

5. Finally, remember, this book is written to remove from our thinking the idea that China is a "blue anthill" of over a billion people; that it is a mass of humanity undulating like an ocean wave, directed by seismac activity generated in Beijing by the few, the unelected, the cadre, and then measured, and often misinterpreted, by the Press whose mind is already set.

As you read and listen to their words, and learn the secret of their survival, may your heart both ache and rejoice as you realize, perhaps for the first time, that China, just like all other nations, is a country of real people who shed real tears.

PART ONE:
IN THE ARENA

In The Arena

An arena is a place where battles are fought, where the air is permeated with the smell and sounds of war. There are the cries of pain, the last words from the lips of the dying, the sickening sounds of clubs pounding on bare flesh, shouts of warning and encouragement. It is a scene not limited to Nero and Rome.

For the past thirty years, China has been such a place. The first part of this book is an attempt to listen to those in the arena. To let them describe, in their own way, the many battles, the many victories.

Be warned that this story is their story, told in their words. Chinese are not like Westerners. They don't set fire to a few adjectives, heat up a few verbs, and inundate one with a verbal conflagration. Their emotions are often held deep inside, not to be exposed publicly—especially to "foreigners."

This does not mean that the events do not burn their way into one's conscience, only that we must listen as they speak.

The Chinese are not quick to tell of their personal experiences. It is not uncommon for them to say, "Oh, I spent 15 years in prison," and then go on as though it was assumed that this is normal for all Christians.

It would be possible to write an entire book on miracles that have taken place in the church in China; details of imprisonment could be presented which would make even the strongest shy away in revulsion, putting the book away to be read another time.

As important as such a book might be, that is not our purpose. Our purpose in this first part is to let those who fought in the arena tell their story in their way.

As they do:

—listen carefully to their words until you begin to feel with them;

—when their words and testimonies become ponderous, stop and feel each event with them;

—when they quietly explain what it is like to survive under terrible suffering, ask yourself the question: How would I do in that kind of an arena?

—see them as people, real people. Laugh with them, cry with them, pray with them, sing with them.

Listen now, to the sounds of battle from an arena encompassing 9.5 million kilometers, with more than a billion combatants.

Chapter One

"A Revolution Is Not a Dinner Party"[1]

It was a cool autumn day in 1966, in the suburbs of Beijing, China. She sat in her wooden chair, her hands folded in her lap. Her loosely fitted, faded blue tunic hung from her stooped shoulders. Her fingers traced what had once been a crease in her equally loose fitting and equally faded trousers. (At 51, one would expect that she is now beginning to enjoy the quiet and gratifying role of a satisfied and fulfilled mother and grandmother.) She glanced across the small room and looked at the pictures sitting in ornate frames on the top of a chest of drawers. Among them was a degree from a prestigious foreign university, and a marriage certificate. Inside the top drawer, hidden under her complete wardrobe (two more tunics and three more pairs of trousers), was a little money secretly saved for some special occasion. As tears began to well up in her eyes, she put both elbows on the small, oilcloth-covered kitchen table and placed her head in her hands.

She could not bear to look across the room at the bed where a marriage had been consummated 26 years ago. Childhood sweethearts had become husband and wife. In this place, three children had been brought into a society that was supposed to get better, but only seemed to get worse. Everything had looked so promising. There was to be no more war, yet their young men went off to Korea.

[1]Mao Zedong

There was to be no more famine, yet there were many days and sometimes weeks when all they had to eat was a sliced turnip.

She knew of the recurring discomfort of standing in line in the cold, freezing winter for as long as five hours just to receive one tiny piece of meat. She would take it home and prepare it as if it were a feast. She would tell her children that she was not hungry and they must eat her share.

Always the officials kept promising that there would never be another "100 flowers campaign"—that terrible time when the intelligentsia were invited to "speak out" against the leadership, only to find that their own voice was used against them as a witness to their counterrevolutionary activities. Whether in prison, or left at home to care for the children, without food, without money, one had to write his confession against Mao. It would be torn up, and another, more detailed, with "all the truths," would have to be written. The mind would finally refuse to operate, and one became a naked target for ruthless interrogators.

"You know what he said yesterday?" She lifted her head to glance at her husband. He spoke quietly while looking out the window into the small courtyard that served as a center for the six families living in the enclosure. "It was in the paper yesterday, in red ink," he said. " 'There is no construction without destruction. Destruction means criticism and repudiation; it means revolution. It involves reasoning things out, which is construction. Put destruction first, and in the process you have construction.' "

"Imagine that," he stated incredulously as he turned and walked to his wife's side. "Put destruction first, and in the process you have construction. What kind of convoluted reasoning is that?" He hesitated for a moment, then reached over and placed a comforting hand on his wife's shoulder. His long, slender fingers, trained to bring music to a nation so in need of something beautiful, trembled. Without looking, she reached up and with her calloused, knotty fingers quietly stroked the professor's hand.

Suddenly his fingers tightened on her shoulder. Her hand

gripped his. They both heard it at the same time. The shouting was unmistakable. Their hands trembled involuntarily. The shouting became louder. For several days now, posters had appeared on their front door. One read, "Lover of Foreigners," another, "Reeducate These Poisonous Snakes."

"Maybe they are just passing by." It was a feeble attempt, mingled with hope—a hope that was soon to die. The angry voices grew louder as the crowd entered the courtyard. The professor placed his hands on his wife's shoulders, then bent over and kissed her on the cheek. He whispered something to her, but it was drowned out by the smashing of the front door. There was a moment of stunned silence as the professor and his wife stared with heartsick disbelief into the face of a former student now standing in front of a crowd half filling the courtyard. Like 150 million other teenagers, the student wore the prestigious band of the Red Guard on her left arm. Suddenly there was a cacophony of voices shouting, "Parasite!" "Snake!" "Mao has sent us!" "Long live Chairman Mao!" "Capitalist!" "Lover of Foreigners!" as Mao's soldiers pushed their way into the room. The professor and his wife watched helplessly, paralyzed by fear and disbelief, as they saw their home being ransacked. She cried out and attempted to stand as the marriage certificate frame was smashed on the floor. But the vicious stare of the youth committing the act caused her to sit down.

In a few moments it was all over. The "flowers of the revolution," arms full of pictures, books, sheet music—a lifetime of memories—and accumulated necessities, carried the confiscated articles into the courtyard and dumped them in a heap. A young girl walked up to the professor. The room became quiet, as if it was an act that had been repeated many times. Without a word, she slapped him across the face. With a cry the wife rose to defend him, but a young man roughly pushed her back down on the chair. She wept as she saw the blood coming from the side of her husband's mouth. Before the professor could ask his former student "why?", she turned and headed out the door, motioning for the others to follow.

As she did, the other youths grabbed the professor and threw him out the door and into the courtyard. The wife, frozen to her chair, placed her hands over her face and began to weep, her shoulders heaving as she cried out to an empty room, "Why, Why, Why?"

Though the Red Guard were not as practiced in the art of carnage as they would be later, they performed their act of destruction and debasement methodically. First there was the fire, then the sound of flesh being hit by heavy shoes and sticks. Next there was shouting, more kicking and obscenities. Then silence.

Slowly, the wife turned toward the door, now hanging on a broken hinge. She stood and with her foot gingerly, almost lovingly, pushed a smashed picture frame aside. She stepped over the mattress which had been ripped open to check for more "foreign contraband." The acrid smell of smoke filled her nostrils as she cautiously peered into the courtyard.

The pile of life's treasures and daily necessities was still burning, but the fire was dying. She saw the face of a neighbor cautiously peeking out the crack of a partially opened door. Then she heard it. It sounded like the moan of a wounded animal.

She followed the sound with her eyes. She froze at what she saw. Paralyzed by fear and disbelief, mouth open but unable to make a sound, she stared at a heap of twisted humanity. It looked more like an animal hit by a truck than her husband. A cry burst from her throat as she ran to the corner of the courtyard and bent over the body lying on its stomach. His arms were underneath his chest, one leg sticking out, the other partially tucked under his body. Gently, she knelt beside him and like a mother reaching out to take her first baby from the midwife, she tenderly turned him over. His eyes were closed, one already swollen shut. Through lips burst open, he emitted moans of anguish and pain. Instinctively, as she had done thousands of times before when she wished to comfort him, she reached down and lifted his hands to hold them to her face. There was a moment of stunned disbelief at what she saw.

She fell across his chest, weeping, holding his two hands to her face; the blood from the fingers, cut open by razor blades, and the smell of burned flesh from holding the fingers in the fire, covered her face and filled her nostrils. They were right. Her husband would never again sit down and with his long, slender fingers, trained by a lifetime of discipline, bring music to the hearts of their fellowmen.

The quiet holocaust known as the Cultural Revolution had invaded another innocent home.

The scene was being repeated many miles to the south where they gathered over twenty YMCA and YWCA secretaries and forced them to kneel in front of the pile of burning Bibles. A large crowd stood around the great spectacle. As the flames intensified and radiated their heat toward them, the victims cried out with excruciating pain. It was a pitiful sight. Tormented by their excessive burns, most of them, including the general secretary of the YMCA, committed suicide by jumping from high buildings. These were the same progressive secretaries and pastors who supported government policies in the 1950s and who praised the party for having attained what Christianity had failed to do in a hundred years.

This litany of brutality officially began on August 5, 1966. The great leader, Mao Zedong, his face sagging in spite of the makeup, breathing heavily from the tight girdle he wore to hide his distended stomach, bloated by his traditional eight-course evening meal, topped by several glasses of the fiery mai tai, traveled from one of his luxurious apartments to the office of the Central Committee in Beijing. He affixed the first wall poster, which was to be a symbol of the Cultural Revolution. It called on the young people of China to "bombard the headquarters" of local party leaders.

Mao Zedong was losing control of the revolution. The party was falling apart from one too many of his great movements "forward," and the old revolutionary was beginning to believe that he was, indeed, immortal. For several years he had devoured all the fawning adjectives heaped upon him by the Western press and academic community. In doing so he became oblivious to the 850 million "nouns" and "pronouns" at home, who needed food, clothing and the other basic necessities of life that he had promised since 1949, but never produced.

The controlled press picked up the theme, and twelve days

later, in the Gate of Heavenly Square at the center of Beijing, a "rally of one million" was held. This was Mao's public call to purge the country of everything old. As one they shouted, "We have declared war on the old world!" "Old" was whatever Mao said it was, with special emphasis on anything Western.

The revolution spread from "Heavenly Square" to the countryside. Within days, 130 million youths wrapped a red arm band around their left sleeve and took to the streets. They were the police, the judge, the jury, and the hangmen. Their word carried no reprieve. They confiscated railroad cars, closed down factories, emptied schools and closed churches. Everything Western—books, records, clothes—was burned. What began as a ripple fast became a tidal wave that engulfed and then paralyzed the largest nation in the world.

Marked for special treatment were those who had been former landlords, those educated overseas, and the intelligentsia. The brunt of the persecution was reserved for the intelligentsia—the very people who had played such a large role in keeping Mao in power.

Furthermore, schoolteachers, college professors, medical doctors—anyone who "did not work with his hands" and therefore a "parasite"—were dragged into the streets, beaten and then made to publicly confess crimes they had never committed.

Old scores, real or imagined, were settled. Street signs were torn down and given new revolutionary names like "East Is Red Street." Attempts were made to change traffic lights so that red meant "go"—in line with revolutionary theology.

Overnight, everyone had a copy of the "little red book" bound in red with a star on the front. It contained the widsom of Mao, which all must study and follow. They couldn't know then that it had been ghost written by a party functionary.

Pictures of Mao were spread across the land. Before meals, families would bow and thank Mao for the meager daily provisions.

The most feared cry was "struggle session." Trucks loaded with shouting, screaming youth and loudspeakers would drive through the streets announcing that a struggle session was about to be held. Attendance was mandatory. Raised platforms were erected in the smallest squares of the smallest villages. The "confessed crimes" of the criminals would be read to the crowd. It could be the owning of a record by Beethoven, an extra pair of trousers, or the undefined "bad attitude" against the party. On cue, the Red Guard would shout for a verdict. People in the crowd were "asked" to come forward to denounce the "criminal element."

Sons denounced fathers, daughters denounced mothers, students screamed accusations at teachers who had flunked them in a course, or in the past had "humiliated" them in front of fellow students.

At a set time, there would come shouts from the audience: "Enough of this; we want justice!" Others would pick it up. Soon they were all crying, "Justice! Justice!" A leader would shout from the truck, "Guilty or not guilty?" It was like a contest as to who could yell "guilty" the loudest. To not do so was to reserve for oneself a position on the platform where one would be required to kneel before the people to receive "justice."

Hundreds of thousands of innocent people were sent to prisons—which were labelled reeducation centers. Many were made to "walk the street." A tall hat, shaped like that worn by a dunce, was placed on their head, and from early morning to late at night, they would walk up and down the street. The other villagers, often their own neighbors and lifelong friends, would hurl insults. The children were encouraged to throw stones at the "self-confessed criminals." There would be a roar of approval when a young child would run out into the middle of the street and strike the body or kick dirt on the "criminal."

As the revolution continued, the violence increased. Mothers stood by as their children were beaten to death. Students who had "bad backgrounds"—sons of landlords, or whose parents fraternized with foreigners—were made to kneel on broken glass and cry to the people to "forgive me of my crimes against you." No one knew what the crimes were. It didn't seem important. It was justice by anarchy and preservation by participation. Families were torn apart. Wives were sent to one "reeducation camp" and husbands to another. Mothers would be left with children to raise, but with no income, no job and no husband. Thousands went to prison, never to be heard from again. Many committed suicide under the constant humiliations and mental pressure.

No one, except Mao himself, was excluded from criticism. Foreign embassies were ransacked.

The minister of the coal industry was beaten to death, while the Chief of Staff of the People's Liberation Army was tortured. Mayors of the largest cities were removed from office and made to participate in public confessions.

Some people, many of whom were now in prison, were beginning to think in terms of "the tribulation" spoken of in the book of Revelation.

The country was being torn apart. Even Mao himself realized that these "little soldiers" were out of control. Red Guard factions had run out of people to "cleanse," so they began fighting each other, adding to the casualty list of those already killed. Goods piled up at docks at major ports. Much needed food rotted in train yards or fields. Factories were at a standstill. The education system was completely torn apart. Books were burned. People would line up for two or three days to get cooking oil, the staple of most of their meals.

The one man who might bring order, Zhou Enlai, was about to come under attack. Though originally and tacitly supporting Mao in the "purging of the nation," he was now convinced that it was not only a threat to the entire social structure of China, but to the revolution itself.

Mao, though already in the early stages of senility, was still wise enough to take the advice of his old pragmatic comrade. He called in the People's Liberation Army and gave them orders to "control the Red Guard." It was what the army had been waiting for and they carried out their order with martial efficiency. Overnight many Red Guard leaders disappeared. Millions of young people were sent "down to the farm" to work with the peasants and to "learn how to provide for the people" by laboring with their hands. This was the seed to what would be known as the "lost generation," as a decade later millions of young people would return to the city without hope or education, but with plenty of cynicism and unthwarted rebellion.

As the nation quieted down and began to lick its wounds, no one could imagine how deep those wounds were and how many had been afflicted. Not even Mao could have predicted what would happen when he allowed his "little red soldiers" to act out the pent-up emotions that he himself had created by his years of inept leadership. The Cultural Revolution, like all of Mao's great movements forward, was now being revealed as not just a natural disaster but one more colossal failure paid for at a great price by the people of China.

In the West there was muted comment, suggesting that it was too early to evaluate the situation and that the movement must be given a "fair hearing" and to do so "we must first start by examining our own assumptions and perspectives." Some would tell their fellow believers in the West that "many analysts held that the Cultural Revolution was motivated not by the fanaticism, but by Mao's distinctive visions of a fair and just society" and that the Cultural Revolution was both "equitable and effective." Though there was, admittedly, "some bloodshed," it was "sporadic and limited."[2]

Those in the world bodies who always look for an opportunity to wax eloquent on the violation of any civil rights were strangely quiet and still remain so today.

Not so the Chinese!

As they slowly dug out of the rubble of Mao's immortality, they would call the Red Guard "thugs, political degenerates, hooligans and the dregs of society." It would be publicly admitted that this had not been the revolution of "newborn things," but rather a "calamity for China" and an "appalling catastrophe suffered by all our people."

The mental scars, the cynicism, the distrust of each other, the personal human suffering can never be measured. However, some statistics are available and they make grizzly reading.

One report on just the Cultural Revolution from China itself tells of 1,700 people of a population of two million that were

---

[2]For an excellent overview on the Cultural Revolution, see *The Wilson Quarterly*, Autumn 1980, Woodrow Wilson International Center for Scholars, Washington, D.C., pp. 106–148.

beaten to death or committed suicide. Of the 750,000 persecuted in Beijing, 34,380 died, including the mayor and deputy mayors of Beijing and Shanghai. In a four-day period in one major city, 1,700 were beaten to death, 33,600 homes were ransacked by the Red Guard, and 85,000 people were driven from the city. All of this must be added to the 800,000 who Mao himself said were liquidated prior to 1954.[3]

How many died during the Cultural Revolution, a period of just over two years? No one knows. But we do know that those deaths when added to a list of statistics that began in 1949 make the holocaust in Europe look like child's play.

Judith Banister, chief of the Chinese Branch of the U.S. Bureau of the Census, used China's own demographic statistics and came up with the following, dealing with one other of Mao's attempts to make the revolution work.

"More people died in China during the period of the Great Leap Forward than in all the battles of First World War, or the holocaust of Europe's Jews, or the Soviet collectivization and Stalin's terror.[4]

"According to one calculation," Banister reports, "the deaths of Chinese from the famine and related causes during the Great Leap Forward may have totaled 30 million people, or nearly double the battlefield losses of all countries of World War II."[5]

Actual statistics of the total number of people murdered by the Mao regime from 1949 to today are not available. However, an analysis from July 1984, from Professor Ansley Coale of the National Academy of Sciences and Princeton University, reported by the Associated Press, says that "about 27 million Chinese died because of the 'Great Leap Forward.' " Professor Coale told reporters that this new information was made possible by Chinese releases of detailed statistics going back to 1950.

---

[3]Fox Butterfield, *China Alive in the Bitter Sea* (NYT Books, 1982), p. 31.

[4]The Great Leap Forward was one of Mao's many campaigns. This one began in 1958 and lasted through 1960. It was designed to accomplish, at a greatly accelerated rate, the economic modernization of the country, with an emphasis on national self-sufficiency and labor intensive methods. Today it is often referred to as the Great Leap Backwards.

[5]*The Santa Ana Register*, May 3, 1984, p. 27.

Remember, the Great Leap Forward was only *one* of Mao's campaigns. These statistics that have been recorded do not include the millions who were permanently "cleansed" after the 1949 victory celebrations in Beijing when Mao declared China a Communist nation. The young people, who were gunned down as late as 1972 while attempting to cross the border into Hong Kong, remain forever uncounted except for the few whose bodies floated down the Pearl River into Hong Kong Bay.

But in the end, they died not by the millions, but one at a time, and that is how we are to remember them.

Chapter Two

"I Will Build MY Church"[1]

In late 1968 and early 1969, as the strident cacophony of the Cultural Revolution began to diminish, there was another sound beginning to be heard across the land. It was totally different from the shrill rehearsed cadence of a million parched throats crying out empty slogans; it contained no shattering screams for revenge. It carried none of the pathos of an innocent person crying for mercy, nor the animal-like moans of the dying.

Rather, it was the quiet, orderly, measured, determined sound of moving feet; but it was unlike those who had gone before, sprinting off in different directions running to or from destruction. It was, instead, the ordered sound of people moving toward a new beginning. There was none of the hollow shuffle of those being sent to places they did not want to go. Instead, this was the measured cadence of an army which seemed to understand their orders and destination.

It was a sound that gained in intensity each day. A sound of feet gently crushing the leaves in a forest, splashing the water in a rice paddy, raising puffs of dust across the dirt road, or cautiously treading on an ice-covered stream. It was often accompanied by singing.

It was the marching sound of an army thought to be not only

[1]Jesus Christ. The house church represents a meeting of believers in a home or in some place other than an official church. It may include many denominations and is not in itself a denomination.

defeated in battle, but destroyed, never to rise again, buried in the ashes of Maoism. The Red Guards had burned their books, closed their meeting halls, sent their leaders to prison. They had severely persecuted those who refused to bow their heads before their meager daily meal and say to a picture of Mao, "We take this meal so as not to forget the past suffering, so as to let you know that our great leader Chairman Mao has brought us today's happiness, and so as to make you become good people nurtured by Mao Zedong's thoughts."

Though forced to listen, they had privately and sometimes publicly repudiated at great personal sacrifice the stories that the reading of the "thoughts of Mao" from his "little red book" had actually resurrected some people from the dead, vexed unclean spirits, and was the creative power in the performance of miracles.

It was an army that was tattered, worn, but far from defeated. They were not returning home from a battle lost, but from a victory won. The walls had tumbled; they were taking possession of the city.

They were the young and the old, the educated and uneducated, the crippled and the healthy.

Some would go to private homes, some into open fields or a clearing in the forest. They would meet at different times, on different days, but when they gathered they all had one thing in common: They had come together to worship the Lord Jesus Christ.

This was the membership of the house church of the People's Republic of China.[2]

Where was the church prior to this time? What had they been doing?

After 1950, all of the Christian churches were to be run by the Communist-Party-approved Three-Self Patriotic Movement. Virtually all rural churches were closed in the early fifties, during land reform. Later in the cities, churches were progressively closed under the pretext of eradicating denomi-

---

[2]The house church is not to be confused with the official church in China known as the Three-Self Patriotic Movement. This will be discussed extensively in a later chapter.

nationalism, uniting the church under Three-Self principles. By 1958, 200 churches in Shanghai had been reduced to 23, and 65 in Beijing to only 4. Many pastors were forced to work in factories or in the countryside. Between 1955 and 1957, there were widespread arrests of pastors. They were often accused of being counterrevolutionary, a catch-all charge, that could send them to prison for ten, or even over twenty years. Many died in prison. Others were not released until 1979-80, and it appears, some never have been released.

Many Christians left the politicized TSPM churches and began meeting in homes. Of course, in the many areas where all churches had been closed, they had no other alternative. Already in 1954, the religious affairs bureau was attacking the "rapid growth of meetings in the home" as "suspicious."[3]

In 1958, in Shanghai the TSPM specifically attacked meetings in homes and free-lance evangelists and "reactionary" doctrine such as preaching the Second Coming. Similar attacks on illegal meetings were made by the TSPM in 1963.

However, with the lack of information available on the church between 1958-66, one did wonder what had happened to the church. More recent reports by house-church Christians tell of it being a time of purification and sowing seeds of growth.

At this time, some Christians heard God's call to begin spreading the gospel in their own local area and to other provinces. In 1958, a group of believers were independently led by God to meet on a specific day at a certain Christian leader's home in southern China to pray about evangelism. After several days of meeting they went out two by two to witness God's love to others.

The coming together of the house church fulfills the words of one of their own who said, "They used persecution, violence, handcuffs, swords, labor teams and prison. They shamed us in public displays, took away all our rights and privileges of daily life. They have closed our churches, burned our Bibles and put our pastors in jail, but they cannot destroy the Church of our Lord Jesus Christ."

---

[3]R. C. Bush, *Religion in Communist China* (Abingdon Press, 1970), p. 211.

One such man was a pastor in Shanghai, whom we will call Mr. Wang. He was arrested in March 1958, almost eight years before the infamous Cultural Revolution. He was sent to a labor camp for ten years of "reeducation." His crime: being a professing Christian who refused to deny his faith. In the labor camp, he continued to profess his faith and to witness among his fellow prisoners. He was dealt with very severely, receiving the worst possible jobs, very little medical care and a minimum supply of food rations. He would be placed in a cell with others whose job it was to make him recant his belief in Jesus Christ. His cellmates would also receive extra labor and smaller rations until such time as they "convinced" the "comrade" to denounce his faith. He didn't, and they killed him.

Another testifies: "Thousands of pastors and devoted believers died because they stood firm on their faith. Additional thousands were sent to prison where they suffered from various forms of torture, hard labor and starvation. The government of China gave an edict to the people of the country, which stated that if anyone was found preaching the "foreign gospel" of Christianity, they would be thrown into prison or put to death. They sent out the secret police everywhere to watch believers.

"One of my mother's co-workers, a pastor, was caught by the Communist officials. They tortured and beat him, trying to make him denounce his faith. He would not do it. At last they became so angry with him that they brought a coffin and made him lie in it. They told him, 'All right, now we want you to make a final decision, either deny Jesus Christ, or we will bury you.' His only reply was, 'I will never deny my Lord.'

"They nailed the coffin shut and left it sitting for a time, listening for a voice from the inside. There was none. They screamed and shouted at him and pounded on the casket. Still, only the sound of quiet, contented breathing. They buried him alive."[4]

---

[4]All the interviews, unless otherwise noted, are taken from publications and/or files of the *Chinese Church Research Center*, Hong Kong; Christian Communications, LTD, Hong Kong; and/or personal interviews with various subjects in China and other parts of the world. Permission has been granted for usage. For additional information on China, one should contact the organizations listed on pp. 168–169.

The persecution which reached its crescendo during the Cultural Revolution was creating a unique body of believers that continued to face the most difficult of circumstances, but with some equally distinctive results, as this testimony shows.

"One time we were holding a meeting of our Christian coworkers, over 300 pastors from different cities and towns. It was to be a three-day meeting. When the Red Guard found out about it, they began to send out secret police to see what was going on. We did not know this. During the meeting, we were praying and the Lord spoke to one of us, saying, 'The situation here is very dangerous and the secret police are coming to arrest you.' Quietly and one by one, all 300 pastors left the meeting by different ways. As soon as the last one was gone, the Red Guard surrounded the building. They were waiting for the 300 pastors to leave so they could arrest them. No one left the building. The Red Guard became impatient and were ready to break down the door. To their surprise, they found it ajar. The room was empty. The Red Guard leader exclaimed more in amazement than anger, 'These Christians are different. They know exactly everything that we are doing.' They left shaking their heads, but no doubt what had happened had made a deep impression on them."

The actual structure of the meeting of today's house church varies according to the needs of the people, facilities available, and that omnipresent party functionary called the cadre.[5]

In some places there may be several meetings per week, planned to meet the working schedule of those who want to attend. Sunday is still the official day of rest in China, and there are more meetings on that day than any other.

Facilities vary. In one small village, the meetings are held in private homes. In typical Chinese fashion, there will be several homes clustered together, encircling a common courtyard. The yard is a general meeting place and may contain the community kitchen and bath. The size of the meeting may vary

[5]A person who holds any responsible position in either the party or the governmental opportunities of the nation. The term also indicates a person who has been fully indoctrinated in party ideology and is a trusted member of the bureaucracy.

from five to ten in one home, to several hundred spilling out into the streets. In some areas, they meet in open fields. Sometimes, the meeting place must change frequently. The time and place for the meeting will be communicated by young messengers or by a nod on the street, or a whispered word in the field or factory.

Everyone in China is organized into some kind of an official unit. The government likes to know if not *how* at least *what* everyone is doing. There are street committees, then block units and on up until you reach the mayor's office, provincial office, and finally Beijing. In the rural areas the people are organized into cooperatives, collectives, and finally communes. At the head of each of these units is the cadre. He is known by many names, not all of them polite in an otherwise polite society, but basically, they are party officials whose job it is to keep their seniors informed as to what is happening in their area of responsibility. There are twenty-four grades of cadre, with number one being reserved for the top party leader, and the lowest, number twenty-four, being responsible for the activity on one street or homes surrounding a courtyard. How zealous they are affects the logistics of the house church.

In spite of schedules, meeting places and the cadre, the meetings go on day and night and in some places seven days a week.

To find a meeting place is not always easy, even if you have the address, because of the great number of small lanes and alleyways. People heading for a meeting, even though they live in the community, often find themselves lost, as this report indicates.

"Our people walked the street, looking for a meeting and praying for guidance. A man carrying pails of water suspended from a bamboo pole on his shoulder came up the street. As he passed them he smiled. A clue right there that he might be a Christian. They smiled back and felt led to ask him how to get to the address they had. The man did not reply, but only beckoned them to follow him. They did, and he led them into the courtyard of a home and closed the gate behind them. 'This is the place you are looking for,' he said with a big smile. 'We welcome you in the Name of the Lord.' "

A visiting Christian from outside China gives this testimony which explains much about the house church—where it meets, order of service, and the impact it has on those who have the privilege of being a "guest" at one of their meetings.

"The hot breeze brought nothing but yellow dust and the smell of sweat. Our bus was moving on a dirt road, carrying more people than it should. I wished that the journey would soon end. Hill after hill retreated from the bus window. So did paddy field after paddy field and those heads dotting the field—the peasants. They had been working since six in the morning and were oblivious of the midday sun. I wondered what went on in their minds while they worked, almost mechanically. Were they bored? Would they want to be otherwise? What did they want? Though Chinese myself, I felt very remote from them. Even the bus I was on seemed to be in a different world than theirs.

"When the bus stopped, the door was blocked by a crowd trying to get on. A brother from the house church was there to greet me. I rode on the back of his bicycle to the church meeting place. We went up slopes and down paths. I was glad I was not doing the driving! Finally, we stopped at a house, where an old lady stood by the door. She smiled as she looked right into my eyes while her hands warmly clasped mine. This was not a friendly handshake with a newly-introduced friend; rather, it felt like an embrace at the reunion of a long-lost friend. I was stirred by the thought that she and I belonged to the same family of God. An unspeakable joy welled up in my heart.

"I stepped into the 'house' and discovered that it was roofless. A sheet of cloth-like material was supported on top of the four blank walls to give shelter from the sun. Yet those sitting close to the wall and the pastor standing up front were bathed in sunlight leaking in from the edges. The whole congregation sat there quietly, sweating. Some waved their fans to keep off flies and mosquitoes. A few children played by the door, unnoticed. I recalled the peasants I saw bending down in the fields, and I could almost feel my bones aching. Yet this congregation, also peasants, sat there quietly and patiently. I felt there was an air of nobility about them. I was greatly moved.

"The pastor started to preach. His voice was low, but there was a thrill in it. Frequently he raised his handkerchief to clear his face of sweat. The congregation responded with very loud singing. Although I was a total stranger, seldom had I felt such an urge to worship God. I felt very close to these sincere worshipers around me. There was definitely more than the spoken language could convey.

"I estimated that there were about a hundred people. When it came to prayer time, they were very open in sharing their personal requests. One of the brothers told of his greatest concern—one of his pigs was ill and he asked us to remember this in prayer. This pig was his food, his bank account, his salary. Naturally and wholeheartedly, they shared this burden. Unconsciously these simple folks possessed the secret of prayer—the natural and honest pouring out of one's heart before God.

"A brother then read a letter to the congregation. It was from a new believer, one of the fruits of the church, who shared that he was in great difficulty and was going to give up his faith. Brothers and sisters responded with prayers on behalf of this sheep. It was a good illustration of the church as a whole caring for its individual members. Evangelism to these folk is naturally the task of the whole church, not just a few concerned individuals.

"The worship service ended. The pastor and many brothers and sisters gathered around us, the visitors, warmly extending their welcome. We stayed for more sharing; we sang our hearts out; we prayed for the church both in China and overseas; and we were even invited to eat with them. As we were leaving, an old lady firmly held my hand and repeatedly urged me to come back and see them. Some brothers offered to give us a 'ride' to our hotel which was two and a half hours' ride away—the 'ride' was on the back of another of those sturdy bicycles. As we started down the road, my heart was still singing.

"When we arrived at his home, I was invited to eat with them. The meal shared with these brothers and sisters was a cultural shock. I was painfully aware of how different my living pattern and upbringing was from theirs. The meal table was placed near the rear door of the house. Sitting there, I could see (and smell) a pig lying by the door. The food on the table was bland, having neither attractive taste nor color; yet I was so busily tackling it that I could hardly free my hands to wipe my face when sweat dripped down. I could not say I had a good appetite, but I felt bad about it. I realized that I had been very, very privileged, up to the point of being spoiled. I talked about suffering, about counting the cost. I thought about missions to China. Yet how successful will we be if we keep on insisting on the inalienable rights or blessings we have, and have already taken for granted?

"The rural churches in China are not without flaw, but I am moved by their single-mindedness for Jesus and for the strong love they have for one another. They have what is lacking in most overseas churches. This, then, is the beauty of the Body of Christ—the strength and the weakness of the members complement one another. With this understanding, we can have a more realistic appraisal of the church in China, and of our place in it."

Chapter Three

These Are MY People

No matter where or when they meet or under what circumstances, the house church is made up of one thing: *people*. Sometimes the absence of those who are *not* there is as significant as the presence of those who *are*.

Missing from the meetings is a young science teacher, a Christian who refused to teach Darwin's theory of evolution as truth. She told the officials that Darwin was anti-God and that the theory of evolution was not true. For weeks they tried to persuade her. Good science teachers were difficult to find, especially after the Cultural Revolution. She would not relent. Her reply was always the same. "We are not monkeys. We are men and women made in the image of God." Later she would cry the same words through broken teeth and bloody lips.

Today, she is a janitor at the school and is forbidden to attend house meetings with her fellow believers.

There is also the noticeable void left by the beloved doctor who refused to confess that Chairman Mao was bigger than "your Christ."

He was beaten and left unconscious by the Red Guard. They covered him with a blanket and let him lie on the hospital floor. They told him they would be back in a few days. They returned and his response was simple, "My Christ is bigger than Chairman Mao. My Christ is the Lord of Lords, King of Kings. He has been given the name above all names in heaven, on earth and under the earth."

More beating, but the same response: "My Christ is bigger." After several days, they decided to end this heresy once and for all. They stripped him naked and made him stand up on a narrow bench, barely six inches wide. "Now," they shouted, "if your Christ is bigger than Chairman Mao, let him save you! Our Chairman Mao can save you; just admit it."

Quietly and barely audible, he repeated the story of the men in the fiery furnace. He raised his voice as he looked at his persecutors and told them, "They were not burned because the Lord stood with them, and He is with me now."

The hours passed, not a muscle in his body trembled. Five hours, ten hours—people began to take notice. "Where does this old man get his strength?" they asked. His very presence was becoming, not only a witness to Christ, but a source of conviction and embarrassment to the others who saw him standing, naked, on the bench.

Finally, the cadre could stand it no longer. Naked, and without a whimper, the "man who believed Christ bigger than Chairman Mao" had stood, balancing himself on a narrow bench, from seven in the evening until ten the next morning. After fifteen hours of what he called "peace and fellowship," he was pushed to the floor. The Red Guard promised him that there would be another day. It came a week later. Dragging him away from his patients, they hanged him.

The Red Guard fought among themselves. They were frightened. Some wanted to cut him down before he died. After a scuffle, one cut the rope. He fell to the floor and preached his last message: "As I was hanging there, my heart was melting for you." He then died, as his predecessor, Stephen, had done before him.

What about those who *do* attend the meetings? What are they like?

Looking across the small room, we see her sitting quietly on a plain wooden bench. Her faded black tunic is a size too big for her, as are her grey baggy pants. Her eyes are closed. Her shining face, framed by her black, "bowl-cut" hair, forms a picture of serenity and belies the difficult road that she has traveled, which has brought her to this moment.

She was only nineteen at the time when her crumpled body was roughly thrown into the dungeon cell. There was no light. All she knew was that it was somewhere underground. The floor was all wet. The smell told her it was human excrement. Rats and vermin were everywhere. There was no bed, so if she was to get any rest, it would be sitting in her own waste and that of others before her. As she sat on the floor, she felt something warm run down her arm. She grabbed it and for the first time realized she was still bleeding from the beating.

Her body began to swell from the beating. Silently, squatting so as little of her body as possible would rest on the floor, she began to thank the Lord that she was worthy to suffer for Him. All she would have had to do was denounce her Savior, but she refused, and here she was—alone, beaten and weeping tears of joy as her cell became her house of peace. Quietly she asked Him for wisdom and strength, not that she would get out of this terrible place, but that wherever He put her, she would be able to continue to preach the gospel of her Lord.

As the days passed, she became accustomed to the darkness. The bleeding had stopped and the swelling had gone down. As she sat quietly singing a hymn, the Lord gave her a message: "This is to be your ministry."

"But," she objected, "I am all alone. Whom can I preach to?" She continued to pray that her ministry would be fulfilled. Suddenly an idea came to her. She stood up and called for the guard.

"Sir, can I do some hard labor for you?"

The guard looked at her with contempt, mingled with surprise. No one had ever made that kind of a request before.

"Look!" she exclaimed, "this prison is so dirty, there is human waste everywhere. Let me go into the cells and clean up this filthy place. All you will have to do is give me some water and a brush."

Not to her surprise, she soon found herself on her hands and knees cleaning and preaching. She was looking into the faces of people no longer recognizable as human beings. Through continuous torture, they had lost all hope of ever seeing another human being who did not come to beat them.

"Oh, when they realized that they could have eternal life, they would get so excited. They would fall down on the dirty floor and repent of their sins, and do you know that very soon all the prisoners believed in Jesus Christ."

When the Communist officials found out what had happened, they were furious. They had lost control over their prisoners. They could yell at them, beat them, and they would only say, "We forgive you in the name of Jesus."

Now it was her turn. They took her out of her cell and beat her, then told her to write a confession.

The warden sent a pile of paper and a pencil and told her to start confessing her sins against the State.

"Lord," she said, "I have done nothing wrong. What shall I write?"

Slowly the words came. Then she wrote, faster and faster. She finally finished and, with aching fingers, handed the confession to the guard to be delivered to the warden.

Soon the warden called her to his office. He was trembling with rage. How dare she write such anti-revolutionary things! He then read her confession to a large group of people. It was the Lord's plan of salvation for all mankind. As he read it, he began to read more slowly and with great meaning. Some were greatly moved by the written plan of salvation.

A few feet away, squatting on the floor is another lady. Her traditional threadbare grey jacket and blue baggy pants make her look larger than she really is. Her eyes are closed. Her hands are folded and held to her lips. The look of serenity that she displays was purchased at her own Gethsemane—which she told about after considerable prompting.

"After several years of teaching, the Communists came and told me that as a teacher, I should not be preaching the gospel. I could have my job only if I would not preach. I would always pray before I ate my food. My cadre leader got very angry with me. He told me that it was superstitious and that I should not pray before I ate. He warned me that if I ever did it again, he would have me arrested. I could not help but thank Jesus for supplying my food, so at the next meal, I prayed. The cadre leader had me arrested and I was sentenced to three years in prison for being 'anti-revolutionary.'

"After the three years, I was called in and told, 'Now is your brain already washed. Do you still believe or not believe in your Christ? Have you thought it clearly through?'

"I could only reply, 'I have already thought it through very clearly. I will still believe in God. I will still pray.'

"I was sentenced to another three years of hard labor.

"After the three years, I was again asked the same question, only this time they were much nicer. 'If you will stop believing in your Lord, we can release you right now, today.'

"It was not a temptation. I simply said, 'I will believe in my Lord.'

"They shouted at me, slapped me about and yelled, 'Your mind is incorrigible; you are hopeless! Your mind needs to be washed even more. Three years is not enough. This time we will sentence you to five years.'

"Five years later, I was again brought before the Communist officials. They were very nice as they told me: 'Now I am really deciding to release you. If you only make one statement, that you don't believe anymore, you can walk out of here, free.'

"My answer was the same. It was no problem. 'No, I cannot.' They shouted and yelled, 'You cannot be saved anymore!' Again back to prison!"

Fifteen years later, she was freed, not because she recanted, but because they didn't know what to do with her.

The service begins as a man, squatting in the center of the now-filled room, begins to pray out loud. Others soon join in. They know that here is a brother who has earned the right to lead such a meeting. His testimony still rings in the ears of many present. It is an affirmation to all the power of the Lord they have gathered to worship.

"It was 1958. For no reason, I was arrested one day and sent to prison for three years. They would not tell me what crime I had committed, because it was not against the constitution of our country to have a religious belief. In 1961, still without knowing why I was in prison, I was sent from one labor camp to another. We would get up before dawn and work with no break, hardly even allowing us to go to the toilet. This would continue until eight or nine in the evening. It was dark when we left for work and dark when we returned, but we would often have to gather for two or three hours of Marxist indoctrination, to 'reeducate our thoughts.' Often the temperature was below zero, and we would sit listening to the harangues while shivering, exhausted from the day's work of hauling stones, carrying a hundred pounds of dirt or rock for a distance of ten miles to build roads. Our food consisted mostly of brans and husks, food not fit for pigs.

"Once I was carrying a heavy load on my back and I fainted. As I fell to the ground, my head hit a sharp stone. When I came back to consciousness, all I could think of were my beloved Master's words, 'The foxes have holes, the birds of the air have nests, but the Son of Man has not where to lay His head.' I got up, put the load back on my back and carried my burden with renewed strength, telling myself, 'If my Lord suffered so, why should I complain?'

"When the Cultural Revolution took place, I was assigned to a labor camp with 10,000 other forced laborers. I then found out that very few knew why they were there, or what crimes they had committed. It seemed so very hopeless.

"Of the 10,000, only 3 of us dared to publicly admit that we were believers. The authorities turned the 10,000 loose to harass and persecute the 3 of us who dared to stand for Christ.

"The pressure was, indeed, so very intense that not one single moment of the day or night was there any let up. When they walked by us, they would strike us. We always had to go to the end of the food lines and eat what was left. We were isolated, not only physically, but mentally.

"But the worst persecution was when 'friends' would try to reason with us. We knew what they were trying to do. One day a very kind man took me aside and said, 'Why do you want to suffer all these things? You have a wife and children. Don't you ever long to go back to them?'

"He could see in my face how badly I wanted to hold my dear wife and children in my arms, and the temptation rose in me as he continued.

" 'Once you say you do not believe in God, at once, we will send you back and you can have a big family reunion.'

"This was a terrible temptation for those who wanted to be free and to join one's wife and family.

"I answered, 'But you don't understand. My Lord died for me on the cross. How can I deny Him?'

"I went back to my labor group and the persecution continued. In 1979, things relaxed in China. Thousands of prisoners were released, but not me. I could not understand why. Finally, in 1980, they let me go home."

Not everyone in the house churches is old or even middle-aged. In the TSPM churches it is illegal to convert young people under 18. They are strongly discouraged from attending religious services. The provincial TSPM regulations categorically state that "it is forbidden to make converts among young people who are under age."

There is firm evidence that sometimes young people (even over eighteen) who approach the official churches to be baptized are reported to their work-unit where pressure is brought upon them to cease attending church. However, despite the intent of the regulations, young people do attend the TSPM churches.

But in home gatherings, young people are welcome. That was why a young girl no more than seventeen was there. Here is her testimony:

"They continued their struggle against me. I was getting very depressed and I asked myself the question, 'Why is this happening to me? I am a good Christian and have never done anything wrong. Why do they struggle against me and not against those who have really done bad things?'

" 'Do you still believe in Jesus?' they shouted.

" 'Yes, yes, I do.' Her depression had gone. She no longer felt sorry for herself.

They took a board 5 feet high and 12 inches wide and tied it to her back. They plastered posters on the board detailing her alleged crimes. They placed a dunce's cap on her head and gave her a gong to ring so that people would know she was approaching. She was like the lepers of old, crying out, "Unclean! Unclean!" On her hat they had mockingly written four characters: "God blesses." They meant it to shame her, but she wore it as a testimony that God, indeed, does bless.

With the tall hat and the gong, she walked up and down the streets, thanking the Lord that she could spread the message that "God blesses."

After they let her go, she returned to her home and in the days that followed many people began to come to her home asking about the God that blesses.

Across the room was a young man, about the same age, sitting on the floor, his crutches beside him. Both legs were stretched out in front of him. A plastic sandal fell from one of his feet as he raised himself up in order to reach into his pants pocket. Finally, he took a small piece of crumpled paper, and with both hands gently unfolded it as he settled back onto the hard floor. His lips began to move as he read from the scrap of paper. He had brought the Scripture for tonight's message. Several months before, he had given his testimony.

"Even though my parents were faithful Christians, I was saved only when I had this accident and became crippled.

"When I was six years old, my father, because of his faith, lost his freedom. In my young mind, I can never forget those dreadful moments and experiences. This has deeply wounded my heart and I can never erase it from my memory. What I went through was indescribable. I had to live through my years with the label that I have a father who was imprisoned in the labor camp.

"I can remember going to the post office to receive a parcel from my father. When the attendant saw where the parcel came from—such and such labor camp—he suddenly produced a different expression. Was it pity, or accusation? I often dreamed of my father. Finally he was released. When I saw him, he seemed to be very different from what I remembered of him when I was a small child. It was ten years since he was taken to the labor camp. He was young and strong when he left, but he had grown very old.

"Not long after, the Cultural Revolution began. I was 16

and had to leave the school to work in the field. It was then that I joined a group of 30 to 50 young people who were simple-thinking and created a lot of disorder around the area. We quarreled, drank, stole and were very satisfied with this kind of aimless, carefree life. We did not realize that this was sin, because we were living in darkness.

"In 1969, after the Cultural Revolution, I came to know another group of friends. They were completely different from the last group. They were cultured and civilized. Their leader would often share with us why man was corrupt. I disagreed with him and would not admit that what we were doing was sinful. I even argued with him. I told him that we did this for a reason, to prove ourselves and to revenge those who have caused inequality in our society. Maybe I considered myself quite healthy, strong and courageous. Yet, there never has been a flower that never fades. . . . This was my 'golden age.'

"In 1973, during an accident, I broke my spinal column. From that time on, I have been a cripple, never able to walk again. Actually, when the accident occurred, the doctor predicted that I would not live for more than three months. It has been six years now since that happened and I am still living—praise the Lord! It was then that I learned to trust the Lord and live for Him. Is this not a miracle?

"People may think that I am an unfortunate person. But I don't think so.

"After this accident, a number of my friends were so concerned with my situation, but no one could do anything for me. My temperature was rising each day. One day a friend came to see me. He was a faithful Christian. I had another friend who was visiting me too, but though she came from a Christian home, she was not yet a Christian. Well, this brother told the two of us to join him in prayer for my healing. Quite reluctantly, the three of us prayed together. After praying for 30 minutes, my temperature suddenly began to go down. This was my first time to experience God's grace, and I felt His healing power in me as I poured out my sins to Him. I experienced and realized that I was regenerated.

"My friends, if I hadn't been so stubborn while I was still

healthy, I probably would not be in this state. For in Psalms we learn that a blessed person puts his delights in the law of the Lord, meditating on it day and night, and in all that he does, he prospers. Therefore, my friend, do not let this happen to you before you come to know the Lord. Yet, even 'though I walk through the valley of the shadow of death, I will fear no evil, for thou art with me.' "

These are His people: singing, praying, weeping, worshiping God.

There is no trace of bitterness, no one speaks of revenge as they answer the question: How did you survive?

"There were times when it was difficult, but that is what it is like to be a Christian here in China. It is a price we are willing to pay," said one man.

"Tell me about it," I urged.

"I was in one prison where we were inhumanly crowded, with ten prisoners to a tiny cubicle. We were not allowed to speak to each other, or doze off during the day. A guard periodically looked into the room through a glass opening in the door. Many fell ill, while others lost their minds.

"One day, another prisoner whispered to me, 'We can see that your religious faith really gives you strength.' This was the beginning of my new ministry.

"Another day, a guard burst into the cell and shouted, 'Stop your smiling!' 'I'm not smiling,' I replied. 'Yes, you are!' shouted the guard. When he left, the other prisoners said, 'Your eyes are always smiling and your face glows with joy even when you are not smiling.' Most of my fellow prisoners were not Christians, that is, not at that time.

"During one period of time, we were sent off to work seventeen hours a day in the rice paddies. We stood in water almost waist high until our bodies were a mass of sores. For a person in his late 60's who was not used to such work, it was nearly unbearable. But even worse was having to listen almost continually to the foul language used by the other co-workers. When I complained to the Lord about it, I felt Him say to me, 'Are you holier than I? I left the absolute purity of heaven to live in your sordid world.'

"Many times the Lord spoke to me sometimes in most unusual ways. Once, when I was young I had a dream. I found myself going up a mountain leaning on the arm of a man. I heard the words of the Song of Solomon, 'What is this that cometh out of the wilderness?' I felt myself leaning upon the arm of my beloved Lord. Years later, I was taken to a prison located in the mountains. As I was walking up the mountain, I suddenly realized the scenery was the same as what I had seen in my dream as a young person. God had prepared me for this walk up to the prison on the arm of my beloved Lord.

"At about the same time that I was arrested, many other Christian leaders were thrown into prison. The scripture that came to me was from Zechariah 13: 'Smite the shepherd, and the sheep will be scattered.' I feared that would happen to God's flock of children. Now that I am out of prison, I realize that not only has God preserved His people in the midst of suffering, but He is sending revival to various parts of China. Now I intend to personally visit some of those revival areas. I see that Zechariah 13:9 has been fulfilled: 'I will refine them as silver is refined, and will try them as gold is tried: they shall call on my name, and I will hear them: I will say, It is my people: and they shall say, The Lord is my God.' "

Anytime of the day or night, any day of the year, anywhere in China—the house church meets.

Chapter Four

The Book of Acts—Come Alive

The more one studies the house church in China, the more one's mind returns to a similar incident two thousand years ago. China was being ruled by its fifth dynasty, while across unchartered desert and mountain ranges sat the little township of Jerusalem. There were "official" churches. They called them synagogues, overruled by a select group of men who were slavishly obedient to a monolithic pagan dictatorship in Rome. But in a stifling, sparsely furnished upper room, a small group of men and women were meeting in a house church.

Luke records it for us in the book of Acts, chapter 2, verses 42–47:

> And they were continually devoting themselves to the apostles' *teaching* and to *fellowship* and to the *breaking of bread* and to *prayer*.
>
> And everyone kept feeling a *sense of awe*; and many *wonders* and *signs* were taking place through the apostles.
>
> And all those who had believed were together, and had all things *in common*;
>
> And they began selling their property and possessions and were sharing them with all, as anyone might have need.
>
> And day by day continuing with one mind *in the temple*, and breaking bread from house to house, they were taking their meals together with gladness and sincerity of heart, *praising God*, and *having favor with all the people*. And the Lord was adding to their number day by day those who were being saved. (NASB, italics mine)

The parallels between Jerusalem and China are as exciting as they are haunting.

A Learning Church

"And they were continually devoting themselves to the apostles' teaching" (2:42).

Believers in China are acutely aware that it is not enough to begin well, but you must continue each day to "run the good race." As the "loud sound from heaven and the trembling of the soul" were followed by a time of special activity in Jerusalem, so the believers in China today feel they, too, are part of a very special visitation by the Holy Spirit. Now they must go on to maturity.

The fear of falling away from the truth or being caught up in a vortex of false teaching is ever present. They are acutely aware of their need for solid biblical teaching and have a vociferous appetite to be fed. One young house church leader, with no theological training, and with scriptural knowledge limited to what he had copied by hand from radio programs, confessed, "My greatest burden and desire is to personally know more about God's Word, so that, not only will I be able to grow, but I can teach others as well."

It is not only the leadership which has this tremendous desire to absorb the Word of God and learn all there is to learn; it extends to the entire body of believers as this report from a house church member indicates.

"Whenever a preacher comes to proclaim the Word of God, Christians gather from miles around. Even when an evangelist has preached to the point of exhaustion, they are unwilling to let him rest, but urge him to continue expounding the Word. In some cases, they have been known to take hold of his luggage and press him to stay a few more days—such is their eagerness to be taught.

"In this situation, where people have been hungering for the truth for a long period of time, it is essential that the preaching concentrate . . . on the Lord Jesus Christ himself . . . the very center. Christians often urge the preacher to help them to come to know the Lord better.

"To give one example, a preacher was invited for the day to a small town to hold meetings. At dawn, the building was crammed with 600 people, with others packed into the courtyard outside. They were willing to suffer the extremely cold weather in order to hear the Lord's message. Before the preacher arrived, they sang hymns in order to prepare their hearts to receive the Word of God.

"The preacher spoke three times and the Christians sat and listened from early morning until late at night. Still they did not want to disperse and plucked his sleeve, saying, 'We have never heard such good preaching.' They were extraordinarily eager to hear Bible truth expounded and to have the Lord Jesus Christ set forth clearly to them."

One itinerant preacher told of sitting down to preach, when the people anxiously asked him what he was going to speak on. His subject was to be about Jesus Christ in the book of Matthew.

"Oh," they replied, "he is going to preach *the* book of Matthew. The entire book is about Jesus Christ." They held him to his word. Thirty-seven hours later he finished a verse-by-verse exposition on the life of Jesus Christ as recorded in the book of Matthew.

Though each house church has a leader or pastor, much of the teaching is done by "itinerant preachers."[1] What are they like? Where do they come from? What kind of life do they lead?

This testimony on the "life of an itinerant preacher in China" should cause us to see that the hand of the Lord is not shortened, and what the old-time circuit-riding preacher did for America, their modern-day version is now doing for China.

---

[1]"Itinerant preachers" are men and women who travel about China illegally in that they have no official government I D. documents which are needed to leave one's own village and teach in the house church. They have received their training prior to 1949 or through the process of experience. Most seem to have a special understanding of God's Word, though many have never seen an entire Bible. Though it is in conflict with Western tradition, these men and women seem to have, in many cases, been simply taught "by the Spirit." Some might challenge this, but to hear them teach would remove any doubt about their scriptural understanding.

"From a very early age, I was willing to serve the Lord, and I preached the gospel to young children. I soon traveled all over—from Henan to Hubei, from Hubei to Shaanxi, from Shaanxi back to Hubei. In the 1960s, I sometimes felt a clear calling that wherever the Lord put me, I would just talk about our Lord. So I knew clearly that the Lord wanted to use me and train me, and hence I was willing to give my whole life as a sacrifice to work for Him.

"Ever since 1967, I have been among Christian brothers and sisters. At that time, Jian Qing (Mao's wife) said that Christianity in China had already been put into a museum, and that there were no more believers. But we brothers and sisters knew that there were those who continued to preach from place to place. Thank the Lord that He has led His people through ten years of turmoil. The Lord by His grace has united and revived His disciples. The Lord has blessed us, telling us that as we do this work of revival, Christ is with us.

"When the church suffers great persecution, I remember what an old believer once prayed, 'O Lord, we ask that you be with us in your sacred work of revival. Thank you, Lord.' Once I heard that prayer, I never forgot it. For ten years now, every time I pray I say, 'O Lord. . . . ' This is truly the Lord's grace and mercy. Although I give very little, the Lord receives my service. The Lord continues to train me and lead me in the revival work as He puts me among believers all over the land. Thank the Lord for His mercy.

"Just now I thought of more words the Lord has given us. The Lord does not give us worry-filled hearts; rather, our hearts are filled with peace and consolation. The Lord loves us, so what can people do to us? He whom we trust gives us strength so that we can do all this. Thank the Lord for His grace. We know we must obey our Lord, not men, because He gives us His precious power and faith. When we go preaching from village to village, the Lord gives us these words to console us. We know that those who trust in Him will be richly blessed.

"We praise and thank the Lord that now the powerful fire of His revival is spreading. The miracles of His power extend to all the lands. The faith in the hearts of the itinerant preachers brings that fire to all places, and then the fire spreads from one place to the next, from one province to another. We can see that itinerant preachers are being used by God to do this kind of work. They are truly the treasure of the brothers and sisters as they do this revival work. They sacrifice everything as they set up underground churches and meetings and call on the brothers and sisters to serve the Lord.

"Several times over the years, I personally have come close to being arrested. Once at a meeting in 1976, with a few hundred Christians, the police came in and ordered that everyone be arrested. We were right in the middle of prayer, and I was with the brothers and sisters praying in the courtyard. One of the sisters pulled me down and hid me. I wasn't sure what was going on since we were praying. Another covered me, and they took me to another place.

"Once a Christian sister told me that in the event of a crisis during a meeting, she knew of a small building where we could hide. If there was any danger, we could very quickly get to this place and we surely wouldn't be discovered. We could eat there and hide out for a long time.

"In another case in 1977, when we were holding our meetings, a party secretary, who was drunk, came and wanted to vent his anger. The brothers and sisters surrounded the itinerant preachers and surrounded the party secretary, too. The brothers and sisters precisely coordinated it; they had bikes that seemed like wings as we fled. Some of the preachers were sent to the mountains to find a place to hide. Some of us were even sent to the party secretary's house. As it turned out, his wife was a believer as well as his daughter and son. They had me stay with the son, and she told her son not to open the door when his father returned. Well, the party secretary returned, but he didn't ask at all about me. That evening the brothers and sisters came to retrieve me and hide me elsewhere.

"Looking at my experience from the viewpoint of the church's revival, I remember that on the eve of the revival, we had asked ourselves just who it is that we believed in. To whom is the arm of Jehovah opening a clear path? We just believed in the power of God to protect our lives. We believed that His work was to be done. I decided to proceed with faith and confidence and the Lord gave me that faith. At that time, there were no churches set up. So we left for Hubei and preached wherever we went. We had the opportunity to share with those brothers and sisters, but they were very poor and I was saddened. But the Lord gave me strength and words. God consoled me and we suffered together. Oh, our Lord is a loving Lord!

"Although we are often cold toward God and refuse Him, our God is still a loving God. The Lord gives us strength to meet with and share with the brothers and sisters. He leads our lives wherever we travel. Although this work is very tiring and our burden is heavy, I felt I must give my feet to God. Once we started, it became a year's service, then two, then three. That was back in 1975. I praise and thank the Lord for His mercy.

"Back in 1973, we saw how the Lord was to carry out His own work in many different places. The Lord used miracles and the Spirit to bring the fire of revival to all these places. As a result, our scope of activities expanded and more came to believe. Everybody was extremely enthusiastic. Wherever we went we were accepted. We were truly moved as we felt their great love for us. Sometimes they wouldn't let us go. We would go there and preach and everyone would cry. We never decided ourselves where we wanted to go. We just listened to their demands about which area needed revival next, and we would go there.

"The brothers and sisters were really hungry and thirsty after the Word in those days, and it seemed that nobody could get enough. I said in my heart, 'Lord, I know too little about the Bible. I feel like a sheep that has to nurse all these little lambs. My milk has already been exhausted and they are still sucking.' I felt helpless. There were hundreds of brothers and sisters in the meeting, and I felt absolutely empty inside. So, I stood up and cried. I said, 'Lord, look at all these people. They came for you and nothing else can satisfy them. You put me in this place, but I really can do nothing. Lord, you have pity on them and have pity on me.' Every time I stood up and cried in my prayer like this, the Lord supplied me with His message out of His compassion for the brothers and sisters.

"During this period, the feet of those that preached the good tidings were a true blessing. Wherever we went, dozens of people would follow behind us and form a big crowd. It was really a moving sight. We used to sing as we marched on the mountain path, whether it was night or day. Whenever we came to a family, the host would do his utmost to entertain us. They felt honored to be worthy to receive a servant of God. Sometimes those families that did not get this honor felt hurt. They thought they were unworthy. Sometimes they even envied those that got to entertain the preachers. Satan attacked many Christians by this means.

"Perhaps I can explain here how we set up these Bible study groups. For those young converts who were desirous of knowing more about the Bible, we organized Bible study sessions on each night of the week for different places. These sessions lasted for two or more hours each time. We first trained some brothers and sisters, and then sent them out two by two to visit the Bible study groups, each on a different night of the week according to a prearranged schedule. It took them a week to complete the circuit.

"In our Bible studies, we follow two principles: (1) to learn basic doctrines of the Bible and (2) to provide messages that are most needed in this generation. As for visiting pastors or evangelists, they are free to preach on any topic according to the moving of the Holy Spirit. In other words, we don't want to formalize or generalize the topics of the messages. In this way our brothers and sisters are always supplied with fresh and vital messages that are most suited for the current climate. After the two brothers or sisters have released all the messages that they are burdend with, they will be led to another cycle, and two from that cycle will take over the former cycle. In this way, the brothers and sisters in all the cycles will always have fresh and different messages to hear.

"As they teach others, they themselves are being trained. After they have been teaching for three to five weeks, or, in some cases, seven to eight weeks, they will have a recess. During the recess, they will be divided into groups and assigned different Bible portions to study. Through this they not only gain experience in preaching, but also in leading Bible study sessions and other meetings.

"After we agreed on the basic teaching materials, we printed several hundred copies of basic Bible doctrines.[2] Now we plan to print the 'Study of the Truth,' 'How to Study the Bible,' and 'Exercise of the Truth,' and then send a copy of each to every Bible study group.

"I am not alone. You see, we have quite a large area to cover, and we have very busy schedules. We feel we have a lot of things to say to the brothers and sisters, especially those whom we don't get to visit very often. They love to have us preach to them, and this overrides their concern for our bodies. We, too, are encouraged by their love; and with the support of the Holy Spirit, we generally don't feel tired when we minister to them. Praise God for His grace."

In order to exchange information and have fellowship and share Scripture, some private pastors' conferences are held from time to time. This is not an easy process. It involves much more than buying a ticket or taking a few days off to attend. The cadre needs to know not only when you leave home and where you are going, but also if you have guests, who they are and what they are doing there. Ration cards, the only way to buy most food products, are good only within your own geographical area. However, all of these barriers are considered to be no more than simple inconveniences.

Recently such a conference was held in a private location. There were no position papers released, no press releases, but one did give this report:

"We preachers always ask the Lord for strength and for clarity whenever we stand up to preach. We want to satisfy the believer's urgent need.

"So far as teaching about heresies and wrong doctrine is concerned, they (the believers) do not feel it is the most urgent need. They still have not clearly grasped the essentials of the faith. Direct preaching against heresy or unorthodox beliefs is

[2]These doctrines included the plan of salvation, the need to be born again, the divinity of Jesus Christ, the need to pray, the study of the Bible (if they could get one), plus other basic fundamental Christian truths.

likely to puzzle them and give them a bad impression of the church as full of strife and slander, lacking in love and so making the church a stumbling block to them.

"The best method is to preach orthodox evangelical truth in a positive fashion—that is, the main doctrines of the Bible, clearly explaining them so that the Christians themselves learn how to distinguish truth from error. One can also bring out biblical teaching as a warning to avoid sin or false doctrine. Particular points which are still unclear can be gone over. In this way, despite various limitations, the believers can be effectively educated.

"In the countryside, Christians usually want the preacher to go over the main point again and again, so that it will penetrate their minds and remain there. So the preaching has to have a wealth of vocabulary to express the message. This kind of repetitive preaching, far from boring to Christians, actually helps them to understand the truth and to make them feel that they have close fellowship with the Lord.

"Today, the mainland needs preachers who have spiritual gifts, who are able workmen and who can pastor the flock. Every message should raise the believer's spiritual and educational level, touch their hearts and build them up in the faith.

"Although the educational level of the country believers may be rather low, that does not allow the preacher to preach carelessly. The Lord Jesus said, 'I am the good shepherd, and I know my sheep and my sheep also know me. . . . They will also hear my voice' (John 10:14–16, paraphrased). All who have spiritual life belong to Christ and know Him. Believers desire to hear His voice, and are satisfied only when Christ is exalted.

"The last few decades in China have shown that, even with a dearth of Bibles and preachers, Christ's flock still desires to follow the Good Shepherd and can discern His voice alone."

A *learning* church not only needs teachers, evangelists and preachers, but it also needs Bibles. Though taken for granted in many parts of the world, a complete Bible is considered a pearl of great price in the Chinese Christian community.

In 1966, the Red Guards made a concentrated effort to burn

all the Bibles, hymnals and other Christian literature. They did their job well. Today, it is not uncommon to see a group of several hundred people with only one Bible.

One lady had a complete Old and New Testament. She would bring it to the meeting wrapped in linen, like the very precious object it is. When the pastor read the Scriptures, he would gently take the Bible from the lady, carefully unwrap it and read the text. After he was finished, he would give the Bible back to the lady and she would wrap it in the linen cloth as others had done to the Lord's physical body.

In some house churches, certain people are told in advance what scripture will be needed for the next meeting. Each of them will copy one verse and bring it to the meeting. When the leader wants to read or speak from the scripture, he collects the handwritten copies, puts them all together and he will have the text. In this way, if the police interrupt the meeting, the Bible will not be lost. The most they could lose would be a few handwritten verses.

Other stories tell of the importance that believers place in the possession of God's Word.

"One time fourteen young people were carrying 1,000 New Testaments to a certain village. They were caught by the authorities. The Bibles were confiscated along with the bicycles they were riding. All fourteen were imprisoned for anti-revolutionary activity, which is a capital offense."

Another reports, "I know of one village where there are 5,000 believers and four preachers, but not one complete Bible. One person has a New Testament which begins with the thirteenth chapter of Mark and goes through the book of Titus.

"Two believers from the North heard that there were some Bibles available in the southern part of the country. They saved up a half year's pay so that they could travel to the South and purchase at least one Bible for their fellow believers to study.

"They fasted and prayed on the four-day journey, asking not only for traveling mercies, but that there would be at least one Bible available when they arrived.

"When they reached their destination, they were greeted with the tragic news that there were no Bibles available. The two brothers began to weep at the sad news. The next day, another who had been trusted to deliver 30 Bibles, heard of their plight and gave them all 30 Bibles. Their weeping was turned to joy as they received their precious gift. They were offered food and rest by their fellow believers, but they refused, saying that they fasted and prayed for the Bibles and they would continue to fast and pray in praise for receiving them as they made their way back home."

Another testified:

"When we have financial problems and then receive money from brothers and sisters abroad, we bow our heads to worship God and give Him the glory. This financial help brings great strength to the house church. Yet the greatest help of all is a Bible. Before, when I wanted to read the Bible, I had to walk more than one hundred miles. I would borrow the precious book for only a short time and then I had to return it. One day someone gave us a Bible. When it was brought into the meeting, we found that we could not talk. Tears were running down our faces. There were shouts of prayer and praise. We handled the Bible with such loving care, thanking God."

Another believer states:

"Because of the coming of this spiritual food, members of the body here have received great comfort. In their prayers, they have shed tears of thanksgiving. We have also offered much thanksgiving to God for your loving concern for us, and we are asking the Lord to abundantly bless the fruit which you have born for the Lord, so that you might receive a reward incorruptible and imperishable. For you have brought us sweet spring water at a time when we were in dire thirst. You have become the Lord's messenger of light to us and a warm spring breeze to our hearts."

In a society where the Bible is available to all, it may be hard to realize the importance of the Word in the life of a Christian.

This letter synthesizes the importance of God's Word to the house church and how they responded when they were given copies of that Word.

"Dear friends, praise the Lord! Today I am touched by the

Lord's Spirit to answer a few questions. I want to tell you how I feel after I received this Bible. I think the heavenly Father really loves me. I am deeply moved and encouraged for you; because of His love, you are willing to help us in spite of the risk of losing your life. At first, I was challenged and revived. Later, I found the way in this Bible and I came to understand many truths. I also see the will of God. Oh! I only know now that I was a seedling without the watering of rain. Now I am like a thirsty and starving man who sees water and food.

"That Bible helped me a lot after I obtained it. I found the way, the goal, and the truth of life in it, which teaches us neither to follow false teaching nor to walk the wrong road. Before, I had walked on many crooked roads. I depended on my own knowledge and wisdom, which didn't work. Oh, I really thank the Lord. He really loves me. Today, He provided this Bible through you to help me turn to the right road from the wrong one.

"I have more strength after I obtained this Bible. No person will be cheated from now on, for we have the correct way to follow. Many brothers and sisters have turned from the wrong to right.

"When I received this Bible, many brethren wanted to have one also. I said that I had only one, but the Lord would give me the second one. I am not the only one who was greatly helped by this Bible; at least 5,000 others were benefited. During the times before I had this Bible, I had nothing to do at home after work. I read fiction, played cards, or chatted with my brothers and sisters. Since I have the Bible, I don't chat with them anymore. I read my Bible as soon as I arrive home. My spiritual life grows daily and the Lord is pleased more and more.

"Brothers and sisters, I want to tell you one thing. Since I obtained this Bible, tens of thousands of Christians are hoping that they can have a copy of their own someday so that they can read it anytime without waiting for a borrowed copy. Now they can't read the Bible anytime they want. They all said if they had a copy of their own, they would read it either at night or in the morning, for there is bread of life in the Bible. Though freedom of religion and Bibles are said to be given in China, in fact, we can't enjoy them. At this time, tens of thousands of Christians come from our province alone, and many are praying with tears about this matter. May the Lord strengthen and keep you.

"Now that I have this Bible, we can make many things clear. People who cried and shouted before have stopped doing that already. Some who were stubborn in following rules before have come to understand and to seek the Lord's will. There were many fake ministers before; now we are able to point them out. There were also many false elders, false teachers and false prophets. The Lord does not forsake us. He opens our eyes and causes us to understand."

The TSPM have claimed to have printed a total of one million Bibles and New Testaments by the end of 1983. This is hard to verify, but many believers report from various places in China that it is still difficult to obtain Bibles. Bibles are on sale only in the TSPM church offices (not the public bookstores) and usually available only to TSPM church members.

Every would-be purchaser has to give his name. In practice, therefore, many Christians in the cities who are wary of the TSPM church, and the vast majority of the rural believers (80% of China's population and probably most of the church are rural dwellers), are unable to purchase them. Large-scale purchases may lead to investigation. For example, a house church leader from Henan in the summer of 1983 approached the TSPM in two cities to buy 5,000 Bibles. In one major provincial capital he was told their total allocation was only 700 and was turned away. (This sheds serious doubt on how available the TSPM Bibles are, outside of major centers.) The same man then went to Beijing and was able to buy 500. However, on the way home he was arrested.

In the rural areas of Henan Province, where the church is flourishing, in mid-1983 Bibles were fetching prices on the black market of between 20 to 30 RMB (one or two months' wages for the average farmer). Even in late 1983, an overseas Chinese Christian reported that his relative, a believer in a town only 100 km from Canton, had been praying for two years for a Bible. She was unable to obtain one until he gave one to her.

This brings us to the inevitable question of the orderly transfer of God's Word to the waiting believers in China, sometimes called "smuggling." It is a subject about which most people have an opinion.

A tourist, a missionary himself, returned from a 17-day tour of the "church" in China, and according to the South China *Morning Post* " . . . missionaries who go peddling Bibles in China are doing so against the wishes of the church . . . but [he] had no intention of handing out Bibles or any other religious tracts." "He agreed," the story goes on, "that there is a shortage of Bibles in the country and that the leaders of the [Three-Self] church recognize that fact, but the church [TSPM] does not want outsiders peddling Bibles."

"I think," this missionary concludes, "it is very insensitive of people to go [to China] and give Bibles out against the wishes of the church [TSPM] in China."

The TSPM has consistently opposed the bringing of Bibles and Christian literature into China from outside. In 1980, Bishop Ding, Chairman of the TSPM, stated that "all missionary and church activities, are expressions of disrespect and unfriendliness."[3]

At the local level, the TSPM states that "we resist the infiltration of the reactionary forces coming from foreign churches. These activities include infiltrations brought about through religious literature or financial or material helps."[4]

In all the discussion of taking Bibles and Christian literature into China, there is one group of people which is being ignored: the believer in China. We know how the Three-Self leaders feel, but how do the believers feel?

Ask them the very simple and direct question, "How do you feel about Bible smuggling?" and you will receive answers like this: "It is easy for those of you who are sitting at a feast to moralize about how to feed those who have no food and are starving."

"I have 3,000 people in house churches that I visit and teach.

---

[3]K. H. Ding, *Call for Clarity, 14 points*, Dec. 23, 1980.

[4]TSPM Document dated May 7, 1983, Fujian Province Publishers in *China News and Church Report*, No. 12, July 8, 1983.

We have three complete Bibles and two New Testaments. What would you do if someone offered you a Bible?"

"Let us decide if there is any danger involved. We can handle it; you just get them for us."

"Why not let us take the responsibility before the Lord as to whether it is moral or not."

"Are we to get a New Testament, tear out everything that Paul wrote? No! Well, don't forget that everything Paul wrote and did for the church was done after the synagogue leaders wanted to kill him, but the believers *smuggled* him out of the city to safety."

The wife of Nobel prize winner Alexander Solzhenitsyn put it very well as she addressed this entire matter of preaching the gospel to the persecuted church. "When someone puts out an empty hand, would you put a stone in it?"

However, the best way to understand this is to stand face-to-face with an old man and give him a simple little present that you could pick up for a few cents in a secondhand store in your country: a complete Old and New Testament. He is so overcome that all he can do is hold it to his heart and moan words of thanks. Finally, after almost an hour of silence, he looks at you and speaks these words: "You must be Jesus, for you have brought me the Word."

There is another book that a *learning* church cherishes. Like the Bible, people in other countries see it so often, sitting right in front of them in the pew rack, that they take it for granted. No participant in the house church of China ever takes a *hymnal* for granted.

Singing is part of worship, of praising God, of learning; and the hymnal is a very precious commodity. Music is an important part of the believer's life in China, as one testifies:

"The hymn 'No, Never Alone' has a special meaning to me. I have been in Hong Kong for just over a year now, having been sponsored by relatives here. People often ask me if I am lonely and how I am adjusting to life here. This song is the best answer I can give them: 'No, never alone; He promised never to leave me, so I'm never alone.'

"Looking back, this song has been a strength to me over the

past years, and I can really sing it with all my heart. I grew up in a Christian home and gave my life to the Lord when I was eleven years old. I wanted to study in the university. The entrance examinations weren't easy. The good high schools of my district managed to get five places in the university, but my school only got three. I was one of them. I felt that was the special grace of the Lord. But things didn't go smoothly and easily after that.

"I entered the university in 1957, which was the year of the Anti-Rightist Campaign. As a Christian I was criticized. They would hold criticism meetings by putting me in the middle of the circle whenever they felt the urge and cross-examine me. After they had questioned me, one of the group would read a prepared speech. When they tired of this, they would send me away until they felt the desire to repeat the same process all over again. I was very much alone at that time as no one wanted to be seen talking to me. Although I was living on campus, I ate alone and studied alone.

"One evening, when I was feeling very lonely and heavy laden, I walked up a nearby mountain. Suddenly this song came to my mind: 'No, Never Alone!' I started singing this song softly, and then louder and louder until joy filled my heart and overwhelmed me. I knew that the Lord was with me through it all.

"The university was 5,000 miles from my hometown. After graduation, I was assigned a factory job and was sent to work in the bitterly cold climate of Manchuria, another 5,000 miles farther from the university. I was a long way from home. I was shifted from factory to factory and given the dirtiest and most exhausting work, which involved long hours—because I was a Christian.

"There was little time to rest. After a day's work, even my family wouldn't have recognized this dirty factory worker. Many of my colleagues contracted occupational diseases, but I remained healthy throughout. For that I praise the Lord.

"I received even worse treatment in the factory than I had received at the university. In the university, I was just an object of criticism; but in the factory, I was condemned as an anti-revolutionary and was treated much more harshly. Again, this song comforted me: 'No, Never Alone.'

"So much for the past. How about the future? One thing is certain: I know I will never be alone!"

In spite of the dearth of Bibles, hymnals, preachers and the difficulty in meetings, the house church in China continues to hunger for His Word. Like those few gathered in that Upper Room two thousand years ago, they are anxious to *learn*. As the beloved physician said of them, we say of the house church of China today: "It is a learning church."

A Praying Church

"And they were continually devoting themselves . . . in prayer" (2:42).

William Barclay, commenting on the characteristics of the early Christian Church, says: "Acts 2:42 tells us that not only did they (the first house church) persevere in listening to the apostles' teaching; they also persevered in *prayer*. These early Christians had a difficult time. They incurred the hatred and the dislike of pagans and were often persecuted. They knew, though, that they could not face all this without the help which God could give them. They were a praying church."[5]

This basically describes the house church in China today. One researcher studying the growth of the house church confirms this as he says: "It appears that the distinguishing feature of the present-day church growth in China is the disciplined prayer life of every believer. Chinese Christians pray to the Lord for (1) a watchful and praying spirit; (2) a burden to pray for others; (3) a time and place to pray; (4) energy to pray with fellow workers; (5) the right words to use in prayer. In this manner they wish to be a trumpet to call all people to more prayer." Chinese Christians have a motto: "A little prayer, little power; no prayer, no power."

It is also important to note how their prayer life reaches around the world. Every Saturday morning, in one of China's

---

[5]William Barclay, *God's Young Church* (Edenburgh: St. Andrews Press, 1970), pp. 17–18.

most important cities, a group of people meet for a day of prayer and fasting. They begin at 9:00 in the morning and pray until 3:00 in the afternoon, or later than that if need be. They do not talk about prayer; they pray—all day. On one day, the number-one prayer request brought before them was that the "Bible schools and seminaries in the West would remain true to teach only the true Word of God."

Here is a group of believers, whose leadership has spent an average of 17 years in prison. Many have only a few slips of hand-written scripture, no hymnals. They meet under the threat of being anti-revolutionary. Many have lost their loved ones; the homes are unheated in the winter and uncooled in the summer. They come together to pray. What do they pray for?

Listen to this prayer from a house church meeting:[6]

"Lord! Revive Thy Church! We love to sing this hymn—it is the cry of our hearts. But before the church is revived, I must ask the Lord to revive me. If every Chinese believer is humbly willing to be set on fire by the Lord, then the gospel will spread throughout the land and shine upon the millions of souls in darkness. The spread of the gospel is every believer's responsibility. Brethren, please pray for me. May we start our work for God from prayer!

"May the Lord grant me the gift of steadfast love to proclaim His love in all its depths. May I have power and authority to proclaim His love perfectly so that the hearers will be convicted or encouraged to follow the Lord with greater zeal.

"May the Lord enable me when lifting up the cross in proclaiming the message of salvation, to have spiritual wisdom to expound the gospel clearly and fully. When lifting up the cross, to explain the doctrine of the cross clearly and to preach its wonders to move men. Oh, for the gift of raising high the cross! Oh, for the power of the Holy Spirit when preaching the cross, that all men may be drawn to the Lord by the power of the cross!

"May the Lord give preaching ability to expose sin, to make

---

[6]This prayer was written by the person who gave it in China and sent by private couriers to Hong Kong where it was translated.

men fear. And the help of the Spirit that men may be convicted of sin, of righteousness and judgment and so earnestly repent.

"May the Lord continually place a spirit of awe in my heart, so that I may obtain humility, and also grow daily in wisdom and knowledge.

"May the Lord grant me the gift of prayer in accordance with the will of God.

"May the Lord grant me by His grace the ability of obeying His Holy Spirit so that I can strengthen my brethren.

"For the gift of expounding the scriptures by the scriptures, thus rightly dividing the word of truth.

"For the gift of establishing and pastoring the church and for prophetic preaching.

"For the fullness of the Spirit.

"May the Lord help me to have a time full of life with Him in the early morning.

"For a life that will be a witness, bearing more of the fruit of the Spirit.

"For more successful training in love, faith, patience and reverence.

"For the gift of comforting people.

"For a willingness to suffer.

"For a gentle, humble, sympathetic, unselfish and honest heart.

"May the Lord control my tongue to speak words that will build up others.

"May the Lord enable me to hate pride, jealousy, robbing God of His glory, all sexual impurity, and lying; and to love truth, humility, gentleness, honesty, holiness, self-control, faithfulness, righteousness, goodness, lovingkindness and mercy.

"May the Lord enable me not to love the world, or its empty glory, but to be bold and be completely committed to God.

"May I have the gift of praising God and of singing spiritual songs.

"Well, I could add more; however, to become such a man is the work of God's grace. If God does not help, man can do nothing.

"In everything we need the Lord (for without Him we can do nothing). If Christ is most precious to us, having Him we have everything. May God be with us, dwell with us and go with us. May God enable *you* not to lose courage, but to fulfill His will. May He increase our mutual love, fellowship and encouragement! Emmanuel!"

A Reverent Church

"And everyone kept feeling a sense of awe" (2:43).

No doubt that first body of believers in that first house church of the New Testament age were in awe at what they had seen God do in their midst. One notices in the house church in China today that same feeling. This is especially true of those who have experienced miracles in their lives.

There was a young member in the People's Liberation Army who became very ill. It is illegal for a soldier to be a Christian. But a fellow soldier, who was a secret believer, became concerned about the man who was ill, even afraid that he may die and go into eternity without Christ. So he shared the gospel with the young soldier, encouraging him "to believe in Jesus and trust Him to heal him." As the sickness got worse, the man followed his friend's advice and repented of his sins, became a Christian, and was almost instantly healed!

When his superiors found out that he had "become a Christian," they began to "try and reeducate him in various ways."

The young man would not give up his faith because he held the Lord in such awe after he was healed. He was finally judged incorrigible and thrown out of the army. Though this would affect his schooling and his employment for the rest of his life, he did not mind. He testifies that he was "too amazed at how the Lord had healed him to do anything else."

Today he serves the Lord with a "sense of awe."

This "awe and reverence" is not limited to the church meeting. It is a part of everyday life. It goes beyond the walls of the house church.

A lady in a major city had a serious cold. Being familiar with the treatment of such an illness, she was about to take some medicine, when the Lord said, "No, trust Me. Just pray and I will heal you . . . just trust Me."

"But, Lord," she argued, "I have already taken the medicine for 12 hours and when you start taking this kind of medicine, you must take it for 48 hours or it will not be effective." She then took the rest of the medicine. In a matter of minutes, she was deathly ill. Never before had she had any kind of a drug reaction. She was taken to the hospital. The doctor looked at her eyes, which were swollen shut. Her lips were four times their regular size. A rash covered part of her face. She was gasping for air. The doctor told her she had had a very serious reaction and that he would give her some medicine to take.

She was taken home where her family insisted she take the medicine. She pleaded, through swollen lips, "But the Lord said He would heal me. I disobeyed Him once. I cannot do it again." They left the room, certain that when their backs were turned she would take the medicine. Through swollen eyes she stared at the capsules on the table next to her bed. She knew they would instantly relieve her pain. "No, I can't do it," and with those words, she took the medicine and put it in a drawer, locked it and tossed the key aside. She lay down on her bed and went to sleep. When she awoke, the swelling was gone from her eyes and she could see normally. The rash had disappeared and her lips had returned to normal.

As she tells of this incident, she speaks in hushed tones, interspersing her conversation with words of awe and reverence.

She is a representative of a body of believers that not only are eager to learn, and to pray, but in the process they hold their Lord in high esteem, speaking of Him in terms of awe and wonder.

A Miracle-Working Church

"And many wonders and signs were taking place" (2:43).[7]

To ask a participant in the house church in China whether

---

[7]A book could be written just on the miracles which have taken place in the house church. I have chosen several illustrations which are representative and are verified by extremely reliable sources. These events are well documented in Hong Kong and personally verifiable in China.

or not he is experiencing events that might be classified as "different" is to invite a quizzical reply, "I don't know what you mean 'different.' "

"Well, you know, things a little strange . . . things that don't happen every day."

"You mean miracles?"

"Yes . . . yes, I guess that is what I mean. Yes, that's what I mean . . . miracles."

"You mean healings?"

"Yes, healings . . . you know."

Let me tell you about a gentleman whom we shall call Mr. Huang, and then you make up your own mind. Mr. Huang was a worshiper of Buddha. His health began to deteriorate until he could not keep any food on his stomach at all. After a thorough examination, the doctor diagnosed his case. "You have a cancer of the liver in the terminal stage. There is nothing we can do for you."

"Mr. Huang then returned to a small town near his native village to await the inevitable. While there he heard about a doctor in the town and decided to get a second opinion or perhaps obtain some medicine that could prolong his life. This doctor was a Christian. In fact, it was this doctor who accompanied the man as he gave his testimony. The Christian doctor confirmed the first diagnosis as cancer of the liver in an incurable, terminal stage.

"The Christian doctor told the man that there was no medicine that could prolong his life, but that if the man would believe in Jesus Christ, he could have eternal life. He carefully explained the gospel to the man and urged him to believe on the Lord Jesus Christ. The doctor also explained that Jesus was the Lord and had the power to heal any sickness if it was His will. 'But whether Jesus heals you or not is not important,' the doctor said; 'what is important is that you have eternal life.' Mr. Huang said, 'I want to believe in Jesus.' The doctor called in another Christian man and the three of them knelt in his office as Mr. Huang became a new person in Jesus Christ.

"Returning to his home, he told his wife of his faith in Jesus Christ and asked her to remove all the idols from the house and burn them. She did as she was told, knowing her husband's hopeless condition. From then on, Mr. Huang's condition deteriorated rapidly. Every night, he and his wife knelt and prayed together. He thanked the Lord that whatever happened to him physically, he now had eternal life. He was gripped by terrible pain. His wife fixed some herbal and chicken soup, but it only made matters worse. In fact, over the next weeks, he became so weak that the family began preparations for his funeral. The coffin was purchased and the grave dug on the hillside.

"One night a man in a white robe appeared to him in his sleep. The man was holding a knife. Not knowing what he intended to do, Mr. Huang struggled with the man in white, but the man prevailed and touched Mr. Huang with the knife. He awoke the next morning at 8 o'clock and was hungry for the first time in many days. After eating a nourishing bowl of egg-drop soup, he fell asleep. When he awakened, he clearly saw two men in white robes standing by his bed. They said, 'You have been healed.' He reached down and found all of the swelling gone. Being extremely hungry, he ate a hearty meal. When his brother came to pay him a last visit, he was amazed to see him sitting up and strong. He told his brother that Jesus had touched him during the night and he was completely healed.

"And in answer to your unasked question, 'Yes, this testimony can be attested to by several co-workers and a Christian medical doctor who has witnessed patients being divinely healed."

The miracles that are common in the house church in China are varied. All, however, are for the glory of the Lord, with all the attendant benefits, such as giving comfort to the grieving.

A grandmother took her young grandson, who was in her care, to the rice field to work with her. There was an accident and he was killed. The grandmother was so distraught, she buried him there as best she could, to protect the body from the elements, and then went to tell the mother and father. The family was gathered in the home, grief stricken at their terrible loss. Suddenly, the door opened and there stood the young son. His explanation was simple. "A man with a white robe came and took me by the hand, lifted me out of the ground and told me, 'Go home. Your mother and father need you.' "

Another incident concerned an old couple who were very dependent on each other. Though they had been Christians for some time, they had no real assurance of what would happen after death. The generations of ancestral worship were hard to forget. One day the husband suddenly died. The wife was distraught, not knowing whether her beloved husband was truly in heaven, or in some state of punishment. She wondered if she would ever see him again.

In the evening, two cadre leaders went to pay their respects to the remains of the old cobbler. As they were standing there, two men in white robes came and lifted the soul—seen in an image—of the man from the casket. As he was leaving on the arms of the two white-robed men, the old man turned to the cadre leaders and said, "Go tell my wife I am going to be with Jesus and I will wait for her."

The comfort that this brought to the grieving wife was added to by the conversion of the cadre leaders.

Some of the miracles are very practical.

A man was sent to prison for his religious beliefs. He had four children, 4, 8, 10 and 12. His wife had to walk the streets with a dunce cap. The children were treated badly because their father was a "bad element." The problem was they had no livelihood, no food. In back of their little home was a small pond. No one had ever fished there before. The children first made a net and they caught enough fish to feed the family. The supply began to multiply. As time went on, they got enough fish, not only for their own needs, but enough to trade for the other necessities of life. Thirteen years later, the father returned from prison. There were no fish in the little stream from that day on. They were no longer needed.

There are also those miracles that not only serve practical purposes, but serve as a potent testimony to the power of God to unbelievers.

A 70-year-old lady in a household was the only one who had knowledge of most of the daily operations of her family as well as the operations of a house church. She alone knew where the Bibles were, who the messengers were, who could or could not be trusted. Suddenly she died of a heart attack.

Her family felt lost. She had not been able to pass on the information that was so vital to all. They began to pray, "Lord, restore our mother back to life." After being dead two days, she came back to life. She scolded her family for calling her back. They reasoned with her. They said they would pray that in two days she could return to the Lord. It would take that much time to set the matters straight.

After two days, the family and friends began to sing hymns and pray that the Lord would take her back. The mother's final words were, "They're coming. Two angels are coming."

This incident caused the entire village to repent.

Miracles also play a major role in teaching and preaching.

"Once I went to a certain county. There is a village there where we gather. The house of one of the sisters was the meeting place. Every Sunday, the Christians would come to this house and everyone would kneel down and pray. After praying, they would leave. Why was this? It was because they did not have a preacher, or Bibles or hymnals and the sister herself did not have much education. So all they could do was pray.

"Finally, this sister said to God, 'God, this kind of situation should not be! You must send a servant to us. If you don't send a servant, next Sunday I'm going to lock the door and not let anyone in. We will stop! I am not educated, so how do you expect me to manage? We have no one to sing hymns of praise. What do you expect me to do? You must send your servant.' But God did not answer her prayer.

"The next Sunday, at the worship time, the Spirit of God filled her. She stood up and preached to the brothers and sisters in Mandarin. When she started to preach, a sister next to her said, 'Don't speak in Mandarin; use our dialect. What are you trying to do, speaking in Mandarin?'

"But she said, 'Impossible. There is a fire inside and I can't control my tongue. I have to speak this way.' And she preached a fine sermon to them. The brothers and sisters were all deeply moved. Also, she sang a hymn of praise very well. After the service was over, everybody was surprised at what had happened and wondered what could have caused it. So they asked the sister, 'Why don't you use our dialect to preach to us?'

"She said, 'It's impossible. About this, I . . .' and before she finished speaking, she began using their local dialect.

"The next week, the same thing happened. The Holy Spirit filled her; again she preached and sang a beautiful hymn. After this happened several times, some of the brothers and sisters began to feel a bit uneasy. 'Is this really the work of the Holy Spirit?'

"So they went to consult an old brother. This old brother was blind but still very alert. They told him about the situation and asked him to come to listen and ascertain whether her preaching was right or not, whether it was really the truth of the Bible and whether her hymn singing was right. The blind brother arranged with another old brother to go to the service together.

"The sister preached as usual and led them in a hymn. After the service, the brothers and sisters gathered around the blind man, 'Brother, is her preaching right?'

"The old, blind brother said, 'Absolutely correct. It was entirely biblical truth. As she preached, she didn't tell you the chapter and verses to look up, but recited the scripture passages character for character from memory. Her hymn was also this way.'

"They asked, 'Was the hymn right?'

"The old believer said, 'Right,' and he told them what number the hymn was and to look it up. So they searched for a hymnal and found that she had sung it right, character for character.

"So many in that area came. Those attending the meetings filled the house, with some standing outside the windows and the door. This was the situation as she preached about the Lord Jesus, and everyone enjoyed listening to her.

"Unfortunately, I didn't ask her name. When I finished speaking there, she stood up and prayed in Mandarin, praising the Lord with 'Praise the Lord; thank the Lord.' I thought it was strange. 'Why does she only say these two sentences?' When others prayed (in the countryside), they talked about things in their hearts that moved them. Why did she only use these words of thanks?'

"Afterward, I asked about it and they said, 'This is that sister.' So I thanked the Lord that this ordinary, rural, uneducated woman was used by God in this way. Why? Because she had a heart of importunity, a willingness to work for the Lord, a heart of love for the Lord. She not only felt a burning to do the Lord's work, but was also like a fire to the hearts of the brothers and sisters who came to the meetings. So God used her and manifested His great power and love through her, drawing many to turn to God. Wherever I went, I saw the work that God was personally doing in the brothers and sisters."

". . . and evil spirits were cast out."

"When I was in ______, there was an old brother who loved the Lord very much and who had suffered much for the Lord. So God gave him special grace so that he not only received the moving of the Holy Spirit and could preach the truth of God, but could also have the gift of healing and exorcism.

"One time, someone asked him to come because there was a person possessed by a demon. No one could draw near him because of his great strength. When the old brother arrived, he said, 'In the name of Jesus Christ, you are not permitted to move.' The man didn't move at all.

"The man continued, 'In the name of Jesus Christ, your hands are tied up.' Then the possessed man raised his hands, crossed as if they were really bound by a rope and could not be pulled apart. Then he spoke several sentences to the possessed man and then said, 'In the name of Jesus Christ, I command you to come out from the man!' The man was delivered and regained control over himself. This incident had a great affect on the people there. They loved to listen to the old brother preach. Everyone called him 'Uncle.'

"From his long experiences, you can see the great power of God in his life and you can also see how God does not ill-treat His servants. He always gives those who serve Him sufficient grace and uses them to manifest His own love and power. It is this way everywhere; you can see how God himself calls and saves. It is just as the Lord said, 'I have come to seek and to save the lost.' He personally has sought and saved the lost. In this trip, I wanted to help gather those whom God has personally found into the storehouse. But I didn't need to use any of my own strength. It was all God's own work and personal action."

In answer to the question . . . "Yes, wonders and signs *do* take place in the house church in China."[8]

When the Holy Spirit visited that first house church in that upper room in Jerusalem, many people came from miles around to share in what was happening. This meant that no Christian had to rent a bed to sleep in or buy food to eat. They would simply go to the house of a believer. Everything that one had belonged to the Lord, so it was a simple matter of making His provisions available for all.

Then, as now, it simply means that if anyone has something that someone else needs, you share it for the edification of the Body. This has nothing to do with a "commune" as we know it in China today. Mao's concept of sharing—you grow it and I'll eat it—has failed as miserably as has all of his great experiments thrust on the people of China.

The house church in China goes past the recent history of China's communes, back two thousand years to that first New Testament house church, as this testimony so beautifully attests.

"I thank God that in our poverty we have experienced the abundant love of God.

"I live in southeast China and was originally a Buddhist. However, I fell seriously ill and the shadow of death bound my soul. Still very ill and in my tattered clothing, I visited the home of a Chinese lady. She not only took no offense at my poor appearance, but later came to see me, showing great concern. Many other Christian sisters also visited me and shared the gospel with me.

"In this way, God used the love shown by these brothers and sisters to lead me to know His love, and eventually I was saved

[8]It is interesting to note that there are no public healing or miracle campaigns in China. Even if they were permitted, they probably would not be necessary, in that these matters are handled within the body of believers, and one does not have to go outside of that local body of the Holy Spirit to see these manifestations at work.

through the precious blood of Christ.

"One evening, at a house meeting, sister Ho brought her five children to the meeting. Only when we finished did we realize that she hadn't eaten. So a brother brought her a bowl of rice. Moved to tears, she exclaimed: 'Lord, you saved my soul and now you give me food! How much you love me.'

"The next morning we visited her home. When she saw us, her face dropped and her children started to cry. We had not realized that they had no food, and not even a cotton quilt, so she had nothing with which to entertain us.

"First we made a fire for her and sent a brother to obtain some grain. He went a couple of miles and borrowed five pounds of rice from another brother. We praised God for this timely provision. After the meal, we went on to another place for a meeting.

"That evening, we reached a common conclusion. The Lord loves us so much, how can we adequately love Him in return? Were we sharing in the physical sufferings of the brethren? Were we caring for their needs? At the close, we all prayed: 'Lord, you love us. Help us to give everything to you!'

"Sunday came—the Lord's day. What could we offer to the Lord? Some brought rice and vegetables. Some brought money. Among them, one young man who had recently been saved gave eight renminbi (the equivalent of one-third of his monthly wages). This brother sold his woolen sweater to an elderly sister and put the whole of the proceeds into the offering.

The elderly sister came to the meeting with her son, who was wearing the sweater she had bought. As the weather was extremely cold, everyone crowded around the stove. But the young man who had sold the sweater could not keep warm in his thin shirt and started to shiver. Then the Holy Spirit moved the old lady's heart and she said to her son, 'Take off the sweater I gave you yesterday and give it to the brother!' He immediately obeyed and she handed it to the elder who gave it to the young man.

"He stood up and wept and could not speak. The other people, not understanding, told him to quickly put it on. So then he explained: 'Don't you know that this sweater was originally mine? But yesterday I sold it to this same sister.' Then the old lady jumped up and cried: 'O Lord, forgive me! I was able to buy the sweater, but I should have given the money to you!'

"From that day on, all the brethren had an even greater love for the Lord and for each other, and regarded the needs of others just like their own. But this is not due to our own power or ability, but to the work of the Holy Spirit in our hearts."

A Praising Church

"Praising God. . ." (2:47).

Listen to this testimony at a meeting.

"What a wonderful, loving Almighty Lord! Jehovah's name is worth praising. His faithfulness goes on for generations. I see with my own eyes that His love lasts forever and ever. As a mother will not forget her infant who needs milk, so much more our heavenly Father will not forget us. Though I have known God since I was young, the pity was that I very seldom had opportunity to read the Word of God. It was like I was blind and could not understand the truth of life. I knelt before God and prayed to Him daily.

"He is truly a God who answers prayers, for things which are impossible for man are possible for Him. While I was thirsting and longing, God provided us the precious Bible through His loving children last year (1981). God's grace should be greatly thanked. Hallelujah! Praise the Lord! From that day on, I studied the Bible every day, and I am enlightened with the truth from the Bible. Countless thanks to the grace of God! Through the teaching of the Bible and earnest prayers, many young brothers and sisters understand that there is eternal life in the Bible.

"Praise the Lord! There is this brother who was put into prison. He refused to stop lifting his hands up in praising the Lord, so he was put into chains and handcuffs along with leg fetters. His flesh was slowly being rubbed off until the bones of his feet were showing. Still he kept lifting up the Name of the Lord. He secretly asked an elder brother: 'When there is a change of guard, will you baptize me?' It was done while the guards and everyone else were sleeping."

Such incidents are not necessarily in response to prison life. There are those praising the Lord while going to prison.

"There was this cart full of prisoners being driven to prison. The people on the street could not see the people inside, but they thought they were awful criminals to be dragged away like animals. The authorities did not want us to see them. 'Are they really that sinful?' we asked. Then we found out the truth. These were Christians on their way to jail. They were all handcuffed together and they were happy. There was no dissatisfaction or resentment on their faces. We could hear them singing as they went by, 'Lord, you are worthy to receive praise. Praise the Lord.' "

An Accepted Church

"Having *favor with all the people*" (2:47).

One thing about that first house church that caused great consternation among the ranks of the established religious bureaucracy was the respect that the community had for them. The same is true of China today.

The key to many of the house church meetings is the cadre. Without his permission, there would be no meeting. Why do they permit the Christians to come together?

One cadre answers that question for us: His superiors asked him why he let Christians hold their religious meetings and he replied, "They are good people. Very moral and very hard workers. They never give us any problems."[9]

The secret there may be the statement "very hard workers."

A cadre's advancement up the party ranks, or even keeping his present job, is most often dependent on meeting production goals. What applies to the local leader carries upward to his superior. The Christians, being "good hard workers," made the cadres successful. It is a chain of events that they do not want to break.

But there are other reasons as well, as this report indicates:

---

[9]Given by a present cadre in personal conversation with a foreign guest.

"In August, a brigade party secretary, who would be a high ranking cadre leader, reported on Christians and had their meeting broken up. Then something happened. He was investigating a brick-burning kiln when it collapsed. He was buried under a huge pile of bricks and rubble. A multitude immediately gathered around and looked on, but the Christians began to pray for him with tears. When he was finally rescued, he said to the onlookers, 'You people just looked on my woe with delight, but only the Christians prayed for me with tears of sympathy. God spared me and now I am safe. From now on, move the church to my house.' "

A Witnessing Church

"They . . . went about preaching the word" (8:4).

From that upper room those first disciples spread the fire of the gospel of Jesus Christ across the world. The parallel in China is remarkable.

There seems to be as many ways of witnessing in China as there are believers.

An older lady, in a major city, has tracts sent from outside her country. Several days a week, she takes these tracts and a pair of glasses that make her appear farsighted. She then climbs aboard a bus. She puts on her glasses and holds the tracts at arm's length from her eyes. Others, as they always do in China, begin to read the tract with her. When she feels someone is very interested and can accept the tract without too much problem, she simply says, "Do you understand what you are reading?" Before the person answers, she thrusts the tract in his hand, gets off the bus and waits for the next one to come along.

The following testimony tells the story of a witnessing church in greater detail and is probably more typical of what is happening all over the world's most populous nation, at any given time, day or night. It illustrates how witnessing reaches into one's everyday life.

This lady and a few Christians who met with her prior to 1948 were members of an existing denomination. Their first house church "upstairs" was held in the early 1950s and continued until the Cultural Revolution in 1966. In late 1968, the house churches spread in an amazing way among non-Christians. The existing Christians who remained firmly Christian through twenty years of persecution had developed the courage, determination, faith, and hope which were necessary to spread the faith. All nominal Christians of the denomination had been swept back into Communism or materialism.

The house church, like most others, is inter-denominational and much less Western in its worship form than the official Three-Self churches which are approved by the government.

"My home is deep in the mountains of northern Guangdong where the population is sparse and life is simple.

"Here we have market days every so often and all the farmers stop work and take their surplus produce to the town fair. They sell rice, peanuts, vegetables, fruit, pigs, chickens, geese, etc., and then they buy household goods. People come and go and the town is extraordinarily busy. They take the opportunity, too, of exchanging news and gossip. But the Christians seize the chance to hold meetings.

"Since the Cultural Revolution, all the Bibles were burned and the churches closed and Christians criticized. But the Christians learned how to do battle with Satan and train themselves, trusting in the Lord. The Christians used to gather at Mother Zhang's place, taking every opportunity to grow in the Lord and in faith, looking beyond the darkness to the dawn.

"I remember Mother Zhang when I was a boy. She must have been about 60 even then. She became a Christian in 1948, and did housework for a foreign missionary. After 1949, because she came from a lower-class background, she got preferential treatment and was sent to work in a children's nursery, but she still remained faithful to the Lord and became highly respected.

"She used to visit all the Christians, who loved to have fellowship with her because she had such a loving heart and was out-and-out for the Lord. If anyone was in trouble, she would come immediately to comfort them and pray. When the clouds of persecution began to gather and the churches in the town came under attack, she quietly prepared herself to be martyred.

But God wonderfully led her away into the countryside when the authorities called for dispersion because of the threat of war. She encouraged the brethren before leaving, from Romans 8: 'Who can separate us from the love of Christ? Can tribulation? Can persecution? . . .' She said, 'Remember, we are more than conquerors through him who loves us.' When she left, everybody wept.

"Life in the mountain village was hard and lonely, but she prayed without ceasing and kept close fellowship with the Lord, longing to find other Christians. One day, when she went to borrow firewood from a neighbor, she overheard a woman talking to her 8-year-old son: 'Who told you that apart from 'class love' there is no other love?'

" 'My teacher told me.'

" 'No! Listen, son. There are many kinds of love. Your parents love you, your sister loves you, and there is a book which says God has an even greater love for people.'

"Mother Zhang then asked her in a low voice: 'Do you have a copy of this book (the Bible)?'

" 'Oh, would you like to read it?' the neighbor replied.

" 'I already have it myself,' Mother Zhang cried happily.

"From then on, God wonderfully knit them together. Through this neighbor, Mother Zhang got to know three more brothers and two sisters. They hadn't had a meeting for three years, but quietly they began to pray about what to do.

"After some time praying, they all decided to meet at Mother Zhang's home, because all in her family were Christians. But, they were still concerned about how they could avoid drawing attention to themselves and perhaps persecution.

"God showed them that they should meet on market days when there were so many people about and the Communist cadres would be too busy to pay attention to the small group.

"Mother Zhang decided to set up a food stall downstairs for the visiting farmers, as there were not enough cafes in the town. She hadn't had it open a month before it was packed with farmers, and they had to increase the number of tables from three to seven.

"All sorts of people came in and she seized the opportunity

to share the gospel with them. Meanwhile, upstairs, the Christians could have their meeting safely because of the general hubbub of conversation down below.

"I first attended their meeting in March 1973. Eight other Christians attended. The bread and nine tea cups were laid out on a table in preparation for the Lord's Supper. After a sister prayed, Mother Zhang preached on 'The Christian's Life of Prayer.' She wasn't a pastor or an evangelist, had no deep theological training, but she was able to emphasize the importance of prayer from her actual experience and testify to the Lord's faithful promises. 'Prayer,' she said, 'is like a radio antenna: it can broadcast our prayers to God and can also receive His answers.'

" 'Mother, we've run out of salt!' Suddenly her daughter's voice was heard from downstairs, using their secret warning. Mother Zhang immediately went out and after a long, heavy silence in the room returned with her daughter. A false alarm! Quietly everyone hummed a hymn and Mother Zhang gave out the Communion.

"Then I explained how they could listen to gospel programs on the radio, and they all burst into tears and praised the Lord. Finally, Mother Zhang gave out the names of the people she had witnessed to, and also news of Christians in other places. The whole service lasted for fifty minutes.

"Later, I received a letter from the daughter, saying the church had grown rapidly to 24 people. They couldn't meet together, so had split into two separate meetings. The new meeting was in a remote mountain village which had six households and had formed its own production brigade. The 40-year-old brigade chief had become a Christian only recently. He led four others to the Lord and had interested three young intellectuals, who had been 'sent down to the countryside,'[10] in the gospel."[11]

---

[10]Millions of young people from the cities were sent to do manual labor on the farms. It was called "sent down to the countryside." They were greatly resented by the peasants.

[11]This testimony is typical of those given in person to a "foreign guest" and is now on file in one of several research centers in Hong Kong. It is available for study by various scholars.

The Secret Church

"Being a disciple of Jesus, but a secret one" (John 19:38).

In addition to the house church, there are reports indicating that there are many secret disciples. How many no one can even estimate. These are they, who, if they meet at all, must do it secretly in their homes. They have no regular meeting time, and they gather with a few family members or very close friends for fellowship and prayer. There are several different types of people who meet in this way.

First, there are those who have been forced to stop attending the house church meetings, or none are available to attend, and are not willing to join the TSPM churches. They prefer to maintain a small, secret fellowship, uncontrolled by the official church.

Second, there are older Christians, especially in the cities, who have been through persecution and feel that because of their past history, it is unwise for them to attend public meetings. They fear it might draw unwelcome attention for themselves and the private meetings which they attend.

Third, we hear of intellectuals who teach or hold positions in hospitals or research centers. They fear that public association with Christians in church meetings may cause them to be discriminated against and possibly lose their jobs. Some of them feel that they can be more effective if they maintain their professional positions and witness quietly among their colleagues. Many are known by their friends to be Christians. One Christian scholar once said to me, "I know all that the Lord Jesus says about confessing Him before men; but for the sake of my family, I cannot at present openly proclaim my faith among my fellow teachers." At the same time, he continued fellowship with friends in his home.

The Growing Church

"And the Lord was adding to their number day by day those who were being saved" (2:47).

No one can give exact statistics on the actual number of believers in China.

To major in statistics may be the wrong emphasis as expressed by one house church member in response to the question: "How big is the house church in China?"

Without hesitation he replied, "As big as this room. Beyond that I am not sure, but does it really matter? . . . Statistics are not important; the quality of the believer is."

However, for those of us who need statistics, there are some interesting indications. In 1949, when the Communists came to power, there were about 700,000 Protestant Christians in China. According to their own recent admission in top internal party documents on religion, they admit that the Protestant church has grown more than fourfold to 3 million. This is a staggering admission in view of the severe persecution and pressure of the past thirty years.

However, there is evidence that in fact the church is much stronger. The TSPM have been gradually increasing their figure over the last few years. Most recently in December 1983, they were admitting that there were 1½ million Christians in just three provinces alone (Henan, Zhejiang and Fujian). And this figure included only baptized believers. The many young people who have been converted through the house church would not be included. So serious doubt is thrown on the official figure.

The Religious Affairs Bureau in Xian in 1983 bewailed the fact that of 1,857 new converts in that city, only 43 had been baptized by the TSPM church. The remaining 1,814 were all new converts who became Christians through house church preachers. One such preacher baptized 179 new converts, and another added 800 to his church in a commune near the city. There is no reason to doubt that the same is true across China. Even the TSPM had admitted there are far more house churches than "open" churches (which now number over 1,200). In November 1983, a TSPM source revealed that in Jiangsu Province there were only 29 "open" churches, while there were over 800 house churches. In the same month a TSPM delegation visiting Hong Kong said there were 50 "open" churches but more than 300 house churches in Guangdong Province.

It is not surprising, therefore, that house church sources speak of rapid growth following the death of Mao in 1976. In

Henan in 1982, a believer reported seeing an internal document stating that there were 1 million new believers in Henan alone. One city there is called by the cadres a "Jesus Den" because 300,000 out of 700,000 inhabitants are Christians. In certain areas of Henan, another believer stated, the Public Security Bureau knows that in every village there are Christians meeting. Believers from this area have stated that in Henan area in adjacent provinces such as Southern Hebei, there may be 10 million Christians. In Zhejiang Province, where again the church is very strong, TSPM sources stated unofficially that there could be 5 million believers. In one city alone there are 50,000 believers out of 400,000 people. In Shanghai a letter from a believer stated that there were ten times more Christians than before 1949. Estimates of the number of house churches functioning there before the recent clamp-down ranged from 1,000 to 3,000. Even remote border areas inhabited by minority people report church growth and even revival. In Anhi Province in one city, a believer reported in late 1981 that there were 70,000 new Christians. Another reported in a letter that there were over 3 million in Shandong Province.

The most conservative estimates of the number of total believers start at 30 million. One group sent an Asian researcher to China where he spent six months collecting church growth information; his estimate—100 million.

These are only statistics. What is really important is to realize that the Lord has wonderfully revived His church at the grass-roots level, both in town and countryside. People at every level of society are being converted, including intellectuals and cadres. In particular, most of the people being saved are young, under the age of thirty.

A Church with a Future

It is a future based on *strength* and *goals*. The strengths are worthy of emulation by any body of believers anywhere in the world. There are five in number.

1. *Bible-based.* All activities are centered on the Word of God. The Bible is greatly prized, with passages copied by hand

from other copies or while listening to gospel radio broadcasts. The vast majority of believers have faith in the evangelical truths of Scripture. The top leaders of the TSPM are generally liberal in theology, but it is the evangelical gospel that has been the base for the great revival of Christ's church in China.

2. *Praying.* Experiencing answers to prayer through thirty years of pressure and persecution has taught many Chinese Christians about the power of prayer. One house church pastor told the writer that on meeting with Christian friends, the first thing they did was shut the windows and fall on their knees to pray together. Many churches in the West have no real experience of living prayer, and could learn a great deal in this area.

3. *Witnessing.* Christians share their faith by their lives and testimonies. Many are burdened to travel at great personal cost from village to village to lead meetings. Others quietly share their faith with relatives and close friends. The reality and assurance of their faith has a great affect in a generally disillusioned society, especially among young people who are dissatisfied with hollow political slogans.

4. *De-institutionalized.* The Christians meet anywhere that is convenient, whether in homes, city parks, open fields, fishing boats, cemeteries (funeral services are a good opportunity for open witness), or on mountains (a good place for retreats). The church is no longer a building, but truly the body of believers among whom Christ dwells. God has raised up younger workers without formal theological training to preach and pastor. In some areas there are quite extensive systems of eldership, pastoral care and training. But the clergy-laity distinction common to institutions has largely been obliterated.

5. *Caring and sharing.* Christians care for each other's practical needs. There is often sacrificial giving to help poorer brethren. Their love and concern even for those who have persecuted them has led to the conversion of Communist cadres.

All the evidence leads us to conclude that in many respects, the house churches are very close in their style of living to the New Testament church. Their love, depth of spiritual experience, prayer life, zeal for evangelism, and patience through persecution are remarkably similar. There are deep lessons here for the Western church, which seems largely to have lost its way and even its message.

The specific goals are equally vital to Christians everywhere.

Recently the Three-Self Patriotic Movement met to set restrictions on "evangelistic outreach." They have called it the "three designates," which includes designated meeting places, designated pastoral personnel, and designated spheres of pastoral activities. It is now forbidden to meet in places not approved by the TSPM, and Christians are instructed not to receive itinerant preachers who are not under the TSPM.

House church leaders then met and gave these guidelines for the house church future goals. Copies of this document have been widely circulated in Hong Kong in Chinese and English.

1. *Preach the gospel of the cross.* Let the message of the cross be spread wherever we go. We must make every believer know clearly that he is saved by the blood of Jesus who died on the cross.

2. *Stress the pathway of the cross.* Our situation is a precarious one. We are under heavy pressure, and many brothers and sisters are being arrested by local authorities. Our meetings are being stormed and dispersed. Our Bibles are taken away. So we see clearly that we have to tread the path of the cross. We must have the willingness to suffer for Christ's sake.

3. *Know clearly the real nature of the TSPM.* Many believers are still very confused as to the real design of the Three-Self Patriotic Movement, and the power of the TSPM is getting stronger every day. In a way, it is good to have the TSPM open churches in the cities so that believers can have places for worship. However, for us in the villages, the setting up of the TSPM meeting points is a trap. Those who fall into that trap can no longer serve the Lord according to the leadings of the Holy Spirit. The TSPM forbids itinerant preachers from preaching the gospel in places where it is needed most. The TSPM also forbids Christian workers from different places to have fellowship with each other. Thus we can no longer hold large meetings. But we are able to hold smaller meetings of 80–100 people at night. We have to meet in different homes each night, just

as we used to before 1976. But God is blessing house church meetings and is opening wide for us doors which no one can close. We thank God in that many brothers and sisters have, after much prayer and fellowship with us, come to know the real purpose of the TSPM and are returning to faithful Christian work.

4. *Build the church according to God's heart.* We are to build the church on the foundation of Jesus Christ. We are called to be builders of His church. So we must teach the people what is the church of Christ. All our work must be arranged according to the biblical teachings of the church, and we must make Christ the center of our church life and work.

5. *Work toward the evangelization of China.* We are stepping up fellowship among Christian workers so that we are linked together in love, and together we will work toward a general goal of the evangelization of China.

6. *Work toward the Christianization of the church.* To strengthen the church, we must have the life of Christ and supply that life to other new members. We must train more young workers so that they can shepherd the new converts and help them grow in their life in Christ.

7. *Pioneer evangelism.* This is the idea of preaching the gospel as we tread the land, claiming the land for Christ's kingdom. Wherever we go, we preach Christ. Whomever we meet, we shall win him to Christ, so that he will also join us. We shall send preaching teams to mountainous and faraway places where the gospel has not yet reached. We are already able to lead people in village after village to turn away from idols to Christ. They then burn their idols after repentance and faith in Christ.

A Church with a Message for the World

A house church leader wrote this letter to the church in the West.

"On behalf of the brothers and sisters in China, I send greetings to the members of the Body overseas!

"Today, the church here is being greatly blessed by the Lord and the number of people being saved is increasing daily.

"The proverb 'When good is one foot high, evil is ten feet high' is true. But the growth in the life of the church has been promoted even by the servants of the devil. Wherever the church flourishes, there are difficulties. The revival of the church here has grown up in this situation. For if Jesus had not been crucified, none today could be saved; if there were no testing by fire, then true faith would not become apparent; and if there were no training, we could not become instruments used by the Lord. If the rock is not split open, the water of life cannot flow forth. So difficulties are the means for promoting life and revival in the churches.

"Recently the gospel here has once again been greatly promoted because ten brothers and sisters were imprisoned, beaten and bound for preaching the gospel fearlessly. They regarded their sufferings for the Lord as more precious than the treasures of Egypt.

"They started to preach the gospel in the poorest and most barren areas. They preached with tears streaming down, causing the passers-by and street-sellers, Christians and non-Christians, to stand still and listen. Even the fortune-tellers were moved by the Holy Spirit and burst out crying. Many people hearing the Word forgot their food, their work, or even to return home.

"This went on until evening and still people had not dispersed. The brothers and sisters preached until they were exhausted, but the crowd would not let them leave. When the shops and factories closed, their employees also listened. However, then the authorities made a move and laid hands on them, dragging them away one by one, binding them with ropes and beating them with electric-shock poles. They also slapped their faces with shoes and knocked them unconscious. But when they came to, they continued to pray, sing, and preach to the bystanders.

"There was one little sister, age 14, and when she revived after having been beaten senseless, she saw that many people were sympathetic to them in their persecution, so she again began to preach. Her words were few and her voice low, but the people could not stop themselves from crying out and then they repented and believed in Jesus.

"When the young girl and her friends were bound and beaten by the authorities, many people noticed a strange expression on their faces, and the crowd saw to their amazement that they were smiling. Their spirit and appearance was so lively and gracious that the people asked them why they did not feel ashamed. They were so young, where did their power come from? They told them so all could hear. Many were led to believe in Jesus by their example.

"At this point, many people who had not accepted the preaching were also influenced and came to watch them. Many people who attended Three-Self churches also came to know Jesus. Those who had not received the truth came to understand.

"When the believers in that area saw the young preachers bound and forced to kneel on the ground for more than three days without food or water, and beaten with sticks until their faces were covered with blood, with their hands made black by the ropes—but still praying, singing and praising the Lord—then they, too, were cut to the heart and wished to share their persecution and be bound with them and cast into prison. So in this area recently the flame of the gospel has spread everywhere. There has never been a revival here before, but through the persecution, this place has truly the seeds of Life. May everyone who hears of this give thanks and praise for the revival of the church in this area.

"In men's eyes, this is an unfortunate happening, but for Christians, it is like a rich banquet. This lesson cannot be learned from books, and this sweetness is not usually tasted by men. This rich life does not exist in a comfortable environment. Where there is no cross, there is no crown. If the spices are not refined to become oil, the fragrance of the perfume cannot flow forth and if grapes are not crushed in the vat, they will not become wine.

"Dear brethren, these saints who have gone down into the furnace, far from being harmed, have had their faces glorified and their spirits filled with power, with greater authority to preach the Word and a far more abundant life. The Lord will have the final victory in their bodies, making Satan to be ashamed. In fact, finally Satan had no way of making them renounce their faith and they were released.

"God has placed us in these last days to wage war so that the number of those saved will increase through us, and that His will shall be fulfilled through us in this generation. He desires us to advance into glory with Him. So making the most of the very short time left, let us continually do the work of the Lord, because there are still many souls who have not been brought home and many lambs wandering in the mountains and high peaks without any to seek and find them. May the Lord Jesus place a burden to preach the gospel on each laborer's heart and give a spirit of prayer to each Christian so each will become a prayer warrior. Let no one in the Lord be lazy or idle. May our dear spiritual brethren strive even more to meet the need of Christian literature, because God has placed you in a good environment to fulfill His task. May God give you a heart faithful to death until He comes. All who have such a heart will obtain a great reward. The Lord will come soon. Lord Jesus, I desire you to come! Dear fellow workers, may the Lord give us hearts to pray for each other, so that we may all be faithful in the Lord's house until that day.

"Emmanuel!"

This letter to the church outside China is simply signed: "From a *weaker* member of the Body, May 6, 1982."

From my padded pew, in my air-conditioned sanctuary, holding my computerized mailing list, an ad for a new version of the Bible, subscription reminder for three Christian magazines, and several invitations to "giant spiritual rallies," I withhold comment—not because of a lack of words, but an inability to speak.

Chapter Five

The Official Church

"And the gates of hell shall not prevail against it" (Matt. 16:18).

The Three-Self Patriotic Movement

Mao was dead, the Gang of Four were imprisoned and the Chinese people began to crawl out of the rubble of 30 years of Maoism-Leninism. One of the new thrusts was to reach out to the world, to put on a good face. That meant that the leadership had to show the world that China was a free nation—freedom of expression, freedom of thought, and of course, freedom of religion.

The Three-Self Patriotic Movement was resurrected. It had its genesis in 1950, at the instigation of Zhou Enlai (formerly called Chou En Lai). It was to be the official instrument that would free the Christian Church of China from all "imperialism and colonialism."

The movement, like so many under Mao, had a life of undulations. It had gained its greatest impetus during the Korean war when its name was changed to the "Chinese Christian Resist America, Aid Korea Three-Self Patriotic Movement." In 1979, it was taken out of the closet and brushed off as part of the "Four Modernization" movement.

Appointed as its public head was an Anglican bishop, Ding

Guangxun, known more commonly as Bishop Ting. He had been a student worker in North America from 1946 to 1951. He returned to China and became president of Nanking Theological Seminary. In 1955, he was consecrated Anglican Bishop of Nanking. The seminary was closed in 1966. It has now been reopened with Ting as its head.

There has been some discussion of his political persuasion, that he might even be a party member. Unlike many other Christians, Ting seems to have escaped any severe treatment from the Red Guard or other authorities. However, Bishop Ting is not the issue. He could be gone tomorrow. His bishopric is as tenuous as any other cadre's.

The real issue is the Three-Self Patriotic Movement (TSPM) itself.

The Three-Self Movement means self-propagating (no foreign teacher or minister), self-supporting (no foreign money wanted or accepted), and self-governing (total internal Chinese control). In the words of the government, it is the official machine "designed to free the Christian Church of imperialistic control."

At its lowest common denominator, the Three-Self Patriotic Movement is an official arm of the government of the People's Republic of China, who, through an appointed bishop and other cadre, is to make sure the Protestant Christian Church is kept free from "imperialism and colonialism."

The purpose of such a movement is not one of church growth, but rather to oversee those last vestiges of Christianity that have not yet seen the light in the acceptance of the coming utopia (Communism) which must be brought about by present socialism. Therefore, there is no evangelism involved. That is why TSPM pastors rarely preach the second coming of Jesus Christ in either the official TSPM church or the house church. That is a theology in direct contradiction to the millennium known as pure Communism which is yet to come. Therefore, such theology is "anti-revolutionary."

The TSPM is not a tool for the expansion of Christianity, but a hammer to pound the last nail into "Christ's coffin." How little they know of Christ, hammers, nails, and empty tombs.

Whoever accepts the bishop's chair has a job description written for him in Beijing. His guidelines are specifically written down for him.

1. Steering the church along the right political lines or, as the party puts it, "guiding the church in the correct implementation of the policy of religious freedom," which according to Article 40 of their constitution states that "citizens shall have the freedom to believe in religion and not to believe in religion."

2. Direct the various Protestant seminaries in China (the main one is located in Nanjing, having 49 students, 19 of whom are women).

3. Keep the church pure from such problems as "denominationalism," which, according to the Vice Principal of the seminary, "springs from the Reformation."

4. Oversee the printing and distribution of all Bibles allowed in China.

5. Oversee and direct the official churches that have opened across China, about 1,200 in all by early 1984.

6. Travel to the West as an emissary of Beijing to convince the world as to the "freedom of religion" that exists in China and how the TSPM is the only officially recognized spokesman for that church.

Is there an authoritative party document that details how the party does this? The answer is yes.

In 1983, an internal circular sent out by the central committee of the Chinese Communist Party stating its policy regarding all religions in China was privately brought out to Hong Kong dated March 31, 1982. It was sent out to the party committees in every province of China. This translation is presented without comment.

1. *Atheistic Marxism is the ideological foundation of CCP religious policy.* Religion is a historical phenomenon of a certain stage in the development of human society. It has its stages of growth, development and disappearance. However, because the development of people's ideology always falls behind social actuality, the old ideology and habits left by old society cannot be thoroughly eliminated in a short period of time.

2. *Religion will ultimately disappear, but freedom of reli-*

gious belief is to be tolerated within strict limits.

In human history, religion will ultimately disappear, but it will only naturally disappear after a long period of development of socialism and communism, after all the objective conditions have been fulfilled.

There will be a time when the vast majority of the citizens in our country will be able consciously to adopt a scientific attitude toward the world and life and will no longer need to look for spiritual support from the illusory world of gods.

Only when we have entered such an era will the various religious expressions of the actual world finally disappear. Our entire Party should strive hard, generation after generation, in order to achieve this magnificent goal.

3. *The Party controls religious affairs as part of its United Front policy.*

Strengthening Party leadership is the basic guarantee for dealing properly with religious questions. The Party's religious work is an important component part of the Party's "United Front" work and mass work and involves many aspects of social life. Therefore, our Party committees at all levels must powerfully direct and organize all relevant departments, including the United Front departments, the Religious Affairs Bureau, the Minorities Affairs Departments, the Legal departments, the Propaganda, Culture, Scientific and Health departments and the Trade Unions, Youth League, Women's Federation and other people's organizations, to unify their thinking, understanding and policies and to share the work responsibility, cooperating closely to resolutely take this important task in hand and steadfastly and conscientiously fulfill it satisfactorily.

We must strengthen the organs of government controlling religious affairs and ensure that all cadres involved in this work study systemically the theory of Marxism concerning religion.

4. *The organs to implement Party policy are the patriotic religious organizations.*

The basic task of the patriotic religious organizations at all levels is to assist the Party and government in carrying out the policy of freedom of religious belief, to help the broad masses of religious believers and the personalities of the religious circles continuously to raise their patriotic and socialist awareness, to represent the legitimate rights and interests of religious believers, to organize and lead the masses of religious believers to carry out normal religious activities and satisfactorily to do all the work related to religion. All the patriotic religious organizations should obey the leadership of the Party and the government.

5. *Only places of worship and religious personnel supervised by these organizations are tolerated. Independent religious activity is largely prohibited.*

So far as Christians carrying out religious activities in house meetings is concerned, they should in principle not be permitted, but they should not be rigidly stopped. Through work undertaken by the patriotic religious personnel to persuade the religious masses, other suitable arrangements should be made. However, in places other than religious places, no religious organizations or believers should evangelize, preach or propagate theism or distribute religious pamphlets or religious books, permission for publication of which has not been granted by the responsible department of the government.

6. *Younger patriotic religious personnel are to be trained in accordance with CCP policy.*

The task of the religious colleges is to train a rank of young professional religious workers who politically love the motherland and support the Party's leadership and the socialist system and who are to a certain extent accomplished in religious learning.

All young religious, professional workers should continually raise their patriotism and socialist consciousness and strive to raise their cultural level and religious knowledge and loyally uphold the Party's religious policy.

The younger workers will be united with the original patriotic and progressive elements in religious circles and will become, under Party leadership, a strong core, guaranteeing that our religious organizations maintain their activities in the right direction.

7. *Internationally, the religious organizations are to fulfill*

Party goals in making friends and influencing people. Foreign religious infiltration is to be resisted especially by the Vatican and Protestant missions.

At present, along with the daily increase in our international exchanges, the external contacts of the religious circles are also developing in a daily increasing manner and play an important role in expanding our country's political influence. However, at the same time, the reactionary religious forces in the world, especially the imperialist religious forces, including the Roman Curia and Protestant missions, are also attempting to exploit every opportunity to carry out infiltration activities in order to "stage a return to China." Our policy is to resolutely resist the infiltration of any hostile foreign religious forces as well as to vigorously develop international friendly exchanges in the religious field.

They must never allow any foreign religious organizations (including the organs controlled by these organizations) to evangelize in any form in our country or to smuggle large amounts of religious propaganda materials and distribute them.

There is in addition to this, the official "Eight-Point Internal Policy on Religion." It states:

"1. Citizens above the age of 18 have the freedom of religious belief. That is, believers and non-believers will not interfere with one another's business and will respect one another without any discrimination.

"2. Adolescents under the age of 18 shall not be instilled with religious faith. But if they want to believe in God of their own will, that is an exception.

"3. Under the protection of the government, believers can have normal religious faith. They should observe all the laws and principles of the government. It is strictly forbidden to defraud for money, to endanger the health of the people and to use public property to set up a church.

"4. It is forbidden to restore the religious prerogatives and systems of repression and exploitation which have already been abolished.

"5. Anyone who acts against the above regulations will be reeducated. If the offense is serious, he shall be punished severely.

"6. Party and League members are forbidden to have religious beliefs. If a member already has a religious faith, he should be persuaded to renounce his faith. In the case of a person refusing to give up his religious belief for a long time, he should be persuaded to withdraw from the Party. Cadres who are members of the Party or the League should not use the authority of their office to promote religious activities. Violators of this regulation will be punished severely.

"7. Regarding people within the religious circle, we are carrying out a policy to unite, educate and reform them. We shall unite believers who have contributed to the Party's general line for the present new era and the 'Four Modernizations.' Those who are progressive and do not obstruct the development of production will be looked upon as our friends. We shall make appropriate arrangements for their living and to solve their problems. Some religious workers shall be trained to undertake religious work in the future. They must be progressive and actively involved in both political and religious work.

"8. The masses will be mobilized to relentlessly crack down on class enemies who are doing counterrevolutionary activities under the guise of religion. Then the vigilance of the believers will be heightened. They will understand the innate character of religion and the proletarian dictatorship will be consolidated" (end of document).

The next question is: Is this directive being followed? The answer again is yes.

According to a recent letter from Central China, the TSPM is putting more pressure on the house churches in towns and villages in the following ways:

1. Requiring Christians to register their names with the TSPM;
2. Requiring house churches within a specific perimeter to be united into one designated place for meetings; and
3. Relocating house church leaders by transferring their employment to another place, making it impossible for them to care for their flock.

Christians facing these problems are perplexed and desire Christians elsewhere to pray for them and to give them counsel.

They are wondering whether this kind of unity is a biblical kind. Many house churches are being persecuted and guards have been placed in front of some of the houses where church meetings used to take place. The guards are there to ensure that meetings do not resume.

This appears to be the implementation of the new policy stated by the new director of the Religious Affairs Bureau, Jiao Liansheng, at the TSPM national Committee meeting held in Beijing, Sept. 19–24, 1982. According to this policy, the TSPM should practice the "three designates: designated places of worship, designated pastoral personnel, and designated spheres of pastoral activities."

Another report tells how the Three-Self leaders, fulfilling the Beijing documents guidelines, controls house church meetings.

"The Three-Self and the police bound the young soldiers of Christ, forced them to kneel, flogged them with electrified batons, and used boots to slap their faces. They lost consciousness. They were not given food to eat or water to drink. Once they regained consciousness, they continued to sing hymns, pray and preach to the onlookers.

"The youngest sister recovered from the blows, and began to preach, in a weak voice, to the sympathetic onlooker. Among those who repented and were saved were sorcerers. Countless onlookers witnessed the suffering and persecution of these fourteen believers. In spite of all this, they were serene and courageous. The onlookers were converted to faith in Christ by the unusual lives of these Christians.

"Those who refused to accept the believers now were touched and actively came to see them. Many believers left the Three-Self. They came to join the Christian band in prayer and sang hymns. In such manner, the church in Yang Chen experienced great renewal. The torch of the gospel is aflame; the unblemished church is revived!

"The young people were bound and forced to kneel for three days and three nights; then they were put in prison. There they fasted nine days and nine nights. This intimidated the personnel of the public security. They were sent to Tse Fang county and Sai Chi county. On the journey, a sister was pushed out of the car. She suffered brain injuries and was in a coma. In the prison of Fang Cheng, this nineteen-year-old Christian sister was released from prison because of physical frailty. She was not happy and cried because her suffering was less than the rest. Her beating was less severe than the others. But in actual fact, she was injured very much. Satan tried to corner the Christian soldiers to forsake their faith. But God enabled them to be victorious over Satan. They were finally released.

"In one voice, the believers of the Henan church uttered, 'Do not fear the one who kills the body, but has no power to destroy the soul.' Lately, the believers in Fang Cheng, Sai Chi and Bi Yang counties were emboldened by the faith of this evangelistic band. Those who did not experience suffering desire that one day they may be counted worthy to suffer for Christ and that the Lord's name be glorified.

"Beloved saints in Christ Jesus, we are left in the world to be engaged in a spiritual warfare with the devil and the evil forces. The Master commissions us to proclaim the gospel to the end of the world. May His will be accomplished in our generation. Then He will bring us to His eternal glory. Therefore, let us labor while there is little time. May we be faithful till He comes. The Lord is coming soon! May we be faithful until that day!"

Another report reads:

"On Monday, May 2, 1982, Lin Xiangao was arrested in Guangzhou. Lin was a pastor of one of Guangzhou's open house churches and is well known both there and abroad. Last fall he became ill, and meetings at his church were suspended. On December 5, 1982, announcements were read in Guangzhou TSPM churches denouncing Lin Xiangao for holding meetings in his home and even entertaining foreigners there. Lin had been in prison for many years and was released in 1979. Legally, he apparently was in a parole period for five years in which his activities were restricted. The announcement of December 5 charged that he had violated these restrictions and was therefore to be justly punished. Although his church stopped meeting after December 5, Lin continued to meet with small groups of his flock."

There seems to be little doubt that the TSPM is taking their directives from Beijing seriously as it relates to the control of the house church.

Bibles, Literature, Radio

Another responsibility of the TSPM is printing and distributing the Bible in China. The TSPM has declared the distribution and printing of Bibles by any other group to be "illegal" or "anti-revolutionary."

Before looking at the actual statistics, there are some interesting articles being distributed in China regarding the official status of the Bible.

One article, entitled "Return the Bible's Original Nature," reads:

". . . during the past ten catastrophic years, not only Christians, but even an ordinary person who owned a Bible would get into trouble.

"The Bible is like Greek mythology and has had a tremendous and complete influence upon the whole of European literature. If we do not have a basic understanding of the Bible when we study European literature and art, or learn European languages, we shall be just like a person who is lost in a thick fog. The Bible recorded religious legends, religious laws, and the works of the chronicles and psalmists of the Jewish people and other races. It also recorded folk tales, proverbs and love songs which reflected the society in Asia Minor and their economy, politics and thoughts in their historic setting. The historical and scientific studies of the Bible have proven that the Bible is not a creation by God, but a collected work done by different authors at different times in different localities. This fact can be seen from the repetitious and contradictory contents and variety of styles in the Bible.

"Throughout history the reactionary class has been using the Bible as the controlling tool. Today, various ideals in this world are closely linked with biblical thought which has become a part of the bourgeois world outlook.

"We should not treat the Bible as devoted Christians treat

it. The divinity of this book which is believed by the Christians does not exist for us. However, we should treat it like any other cultural heritage and we should study, criticize and analyze it from the perspective of the materialistic and scientific attitude" (by Chi, Ben Yu from *Reading*, Vol. 9, 1980).

In an article in the *History of Western Literature*, there is an even sharper criticism of the Bible. The author of the article is the editor for textbooks in twenty-four of the higher educational institutes including some of the best-known universities, so obviously he has the support of the government in what he writes. The writer says:

> The Old Testament has included all the essence and achievement of the ancient Hebrew literature. The New Testament is the Christian scripture for propagating Christianity. . . . Genesis is a collection of mythology and legends.
>
> The Old Testament is the scripture of Judaism, and is a part of the Christian Bible. Its propagation of religious idealism has poisoned many people's minds and caused corruption and damage to human lives. Therefore, we have to analyze and criticize it from the viewpoint of Marxism and Leninism (by Gi Ling Publication).

It is obvious that members of the Communist government realize that in maintaining relationships with the Western world and studying Western culture, they must accept the presence of the Bible. However, they seek to minimize its influence by criticizing its contents. Sometimes Communist writers have taken quotations from the Bible out of context. Jesus' words in Matthew 10:34, "Do not think that I have come to bring peace on earth. I have not come to bring peace but a sword," is quoted in order to make out that Jesus was a warmonger. In the past, leaders of the TSPM have taken Jesus' criticism of the scribes and Pharisees in Matthew 23 as justification for accusation meetings in the churches ("How to Hold a Successful Accusation Meeting," by Liu Linag Mo, YMCA, Sec. 1951; "Religious Policy and Practice in Communist China," by Donald E. McInnis). More recently a university journal had an article entitled "The Original Christianity—Enslavement and Feudalism." It used Luke 16:16, "The law and the prophets were until John; since then the good news of the kingdom of God is preached, and every one enters it violently" (RSV). They use this scripture to support a misinterpretation ("The kingdom of God requires violence to enter it" by Che, Min Zhou, *Nankai Journal*, Tienjin).

As for printing and distributing of the Bible, statistics are sketchy.

The official organ of the Beijing government, the *New China News Agency*, says that "260,000 Bibles (will be) printed in 1982," with a projected goal of 600,000 for 1983. This can be added to the 135,000 Bibles and New Testaments that are not "officially in print."

One is reminded that the population of the People's Republic of China is over one billion people.

Not only is the TSPM responsible for printing all Bibles in China, but all other Christian literature as well.

A limited quantity of hymnals, sermons and devotional material have been published by the TSPM but are clearly inadequate to meet the demands. No evangelistic or children's materials are allowed by the party to be published. In many areas, and even major cities such as Shanghai, believers in 1983 were mimeographing books and booklets because of the lack of Christian literature available. Many have written appreciative letters to Christian groups outside China sending in such materials.

The totality of control of Christianity by the TSPM encompasses not only the official churches now open in the major cities (staffed by 5,900 registered pastors and preachers), the printing and distribution of all religious reading materials, but they also want to control what people listen to on radio.

It has been reported that posters have appeared in Henan Province that forbids listening to "reactionary" broadcasts. Apparently the regulation is directed against Christians. Henan is the province where Christians are most numerous and active, and there is no other social peculiarity which would lead to the forbidding of listening to radio broadcasts.

In another report, a Christian traveler reported that in one of the TSPM churches in Shanghai, it was publicly announced that Christian radio broadcasting is hostile in character and believers were urged not to listen to such programs.

In late 1983, a young man in Manchuria wrote to a Christian gospel broadcasting organization requesting a Bible. The letter was opened and he was publicly criticized by his school authorities.

The TSPM has support of a Western source, as indicated by a report from Hong Kong that the Lutheran World Federation Commission on Communications has declined a suggestion that it consider broadcasting Christian programs to China. The commission heard testimony from an LWF delegation to China that indicated that broadcasting was not in keeping with the Three-Self principle of the churches. The Commission accepted this advice unanimously, rejecting testimony that the Christian populace of China were in favor of broadcasts in spite of the Three-Self leadership.

Another area of responsibility of the TSPM is the total control of the official churches. These are the ones all tourists, from Jimmy Carter to the John Does, visit.

The typical Western "tourist" is not always aware that things are not always what they seem in the TSPM churches. This is not surprising. Most Westerners do not speak Chinese and have no opportunity to talk to Chinese Christians freely. Their contact with the Chinese church is limited to talks with the TSPM pastors and officials. Often they are even led to special foreigners' galleries where they are segregated from the ordinary Chinese believers. Very few are able to meet Chinese Christians in their homes. However, behind the official facade, many Chinese believers report a very different picture. Believers in both house churches and TSPM churches are often under surveillance. In each TSPM church, there are officials (they may be pastors, interpreters or ushers) whose job it is to report anything out of the ordinary to the authorities and even intervene themselves in certain circumstances.

For instance, one lady who attends a TSPM church, but is also very active in the house churches, said that after having a long conversation with a foreigner, she was rebuked by a pastor and told she should only give a brief greeting and not engage in detailed conversation with foreigners. Foreign Christian residents in China who know the language will often report being followed up the street after they have left a TSPM church with some young Chinese friends. The Chinese themselves have later told them that it took them an hour to lose those who were following them.

There are several known cases where TSPM pastors or officials have reported "illegal" activities to the police. In one case, a believer mentioned to a supposedly trustworthy TSPM pastor that he had received Christian literature from some visitors. Soon after, he was detained by the police and interrogated. In another case in 1983, a foreign visitor mentioned casually to a TSPM pastor that she was going to see a particular Christian in his home. After she left, the believer was arrested and some Christian literature she had given him was confiscated. Many times Christian visitors report being interrupted by TSPM officials when talking to Chinese Christians. Those who do not leave quickly are often asked to give their name and work-unit.

In early 1983, a faithful TSPM pastor was leading a young people's Bible study on Genesis. But after two months, he was stopped by TSPM officials in his own church. The reason they gave was that Genesis opposes the Marxist dogma that "labor created the world" rather than God, and he was opposing the theory of evolution by stressing creation. Further, they were unhappy about him influencing the children of other TSPM pastors in the church who were modernists.

In another city in 1983, a visitor gave out some Christian literature which was gladly received by some of the congregation. After he had left, one of the TSPM pastors demanded that it all be handed back to him. Some TSPM pastors preach the gospel from their pulpits. However, even excellent preaching is not necessarily proof that that person is spiritually reliable. One Westerner heard an excellent sermon. However, afterward he was told privately by Christians that that particular TSPM pastor had betrayed many Christians. Ultimately, only Chinese believers know the full story of what goes on behind the scenes in some TSPM churches.

Ironically, though an avowed purpose of the TSPM is to rid

the church of "western ideology," the TSPM in general is structured on traditional Western lines, whereas the house church is not. For example, the house churches have developed new forms of lay ministry, while the TSPM maintain the clergy-laity distinction.

Not All Sinners, Not All Saints

In all things, there are two sides. One may outweigh the other, but both sides should still be examined.

Not all the TSPM is negative. There are several aspects that remind us that the Lord's ways are not always our ways, and that He can use men in different ways and for many different purposes.

1. There are approximately 5,900 registered pastors and preachers in the official TSPM. Most of them are 60 years of age. Many are in poor health, having been imprisoned for long years. There can be little doubt that many of them are outstanding Christians, who feel that this is a place where the Lord has placed them to minister. There is no reason to believe that they are wrong. It is a very difficult assignment, and many would prefer to be out in the countryside where the church is flourishing. It is not uncommon to hear a solid evangelical message from the pulpit of the Three-Self churches. There are those who are influenced by the gospel by attending these services. By allowing these churches to remain open, the government is, in effect, propagating the gospel of Jesus Christ. The very thing to which they are opposed.

2. When the official churches were reopened in the early eighties, it was assumed that they would simply be a token place of worship for tourists and a few old people. However, on the first Sunday morning, they were proven wrong. Thousands flocked to the services, and they were not tourists. Men and women of all ages wept as they sang "Zion Stands on Hills Surrounded" and heard for the first time in many years God's Word read to them from a real pulpit. The very existence of the "official" churches, which shows that the party cannot ignore the growing Christian Church, serves as a ringing affirmation

that the church was and is very much alive. It is a great testimony to the power of the gospel, as it is to the bankruptcy of Marxism, to win the minds and hearts of China.

As the *Far East Economic Review* reported in an article on what they called the "Born-Again" movement in China, "It [the Three-Self Movement] is part of its [Beijing] rationale indicating that Marxism cannot fill voids in the thinking process of man, but rather creates them." A party official pointed out, "God is a basic human need that cannot be ignored indefinitely." A strange statement for a Marxist leader.

3. In God's providence, the TSPM does provide a barrier against misguided Western Christians with more zeal than knowledge. God has broken down many denominational barriers in China over the last thirty years, and it would be tragic if Western missions were to resurrect them.

The evidence seems to overwhelmingly indicate that the body of believers in China will continue to grow: (1) in spite of the TSPM; (2) because of the house church, as the Holy Spirit so directs, according to the hearts of the believers.

In light of these problems, there are two things that are suggested by Christians in China.

The house church is aware of the spiritual nature of the battle in which they are involved. They realize that "not by might nor by power, but by the Spirit of God" (Zech. 4:6) will the house church fulfill its function. The house church has launched out against the problems in this Body.

As for the Three-Self Patriotic Movement, in the September 1981, issue of their magazine *Heavenly Wind*, they answer the question for us. "Today as we rebuild our church, to organize our church, do we really need to preach a message of healing and miracles?"

Their startling answer: "This is not in accordance with the teaching of Christ . . . [signs and wonders] are non-scientific, and only create superstition." This gives the TSPM church license not only to forbid so much of the work of the Holy Spirit in the official church, but in the house church as well, branding all excesses as part and parcel of the ordinary, which it is not. The believers in China simply respond, "He has not brought us this far to let us go now."

Chapter Six

Before Leaving the Arena

As we move from the arena to the spectators' stands, leaving behind the sweat of battle for the comfort of the grandstands, it might be well to allow some of the participants one more word which would synopsize the battle.

Today's Chinese:

"We are survivors. We were once bitten by the tiger, but it failed to grind us small enough to swallow. Its claws left scars on our faces, so we are not handsome."

A Party Official:

"Some patriotic high intellectuals with a good knowledge of religion must be trained. They are useful for promoting an international united front and for contacts abroad."

The Head of the TSPM Church:

"We do not think this big numerical growth (of the Chinese church) should or can continue because it is already larger than our work of Christian nurture can cope with."

Western Journalist:

"The move to wipe out religion in China has failed."

House Church Members:

"The more they mistreat me, the greater the blessing from the Lord."

"As for our pastors, each has served an average of 17 years and three months in prison for his faith, much of it in solitary confinement."

"Don't come into this meeting [of a house church] to talk about or do anything that you are not willing to die for."

"To accept baptism is to mean you are saying publicly that you are ready to die for the Lord Jesus Christ."

Young Marxist Student (University):

"China wants us to struggle against each other, against heaven, against earth, against man. I'm tired of the struggle. I want to love."

Founder of the House Church:

"I will build *My* church, and the gates of hell shall not prevail against it!"

PART TWO:

IN THE SPECTATORS' STANDS

In the Spectators' Stands

There is a great difference between being down in the arena as a participant and sitting in the stands as a spectator.

As spectators, all we have to do is show up, watch, and then leave, perhaps no different a person than when we entered. We don't have to go through a grueling preparation, let alone pay the price of battle. We don't even have to get our clothes wrinkled.

However, perhaps in some small way, a spectator can think upon the scenes he has witnessed in the arena, and then make a reasonable attempt to bring them together in some meaningful observations.

The second part of this book is an earnest, though perhaps somewhat feeble, attempt to accomplish that task.

Chapter Seven

How the Church Survived

There are probably as many reasons and illustrations for the survival and growth of the church in China as there are people in that country.

However, there are some general observations that can be extremely helpful in assessing the reasons for the impressive display of the work of the Holy Spirit among believers and non-believers during the past three decades of Communist control.

Though not necessarily listed in their order of importance, they are:

1. *Intercessory prayer.* There has been much written about the missionary exodus from China during the early years of the Communist occupation. What is often ignored is the simple fact that many of those who left China on their knees never got up. They left physically but never spiritually.

They were not defeated; they simply continued to do battle in one of the toughest arenas of all: intercessory prayer. They were often maligned for not realizing that this was a "different world we live in, and there is nothing you can do for China." Few were (or have been) recognized for their contribution to the building of His kingdom. They nevertheless continued hour by hour, day by day, and year by year, remembering by name those they left behind in the villages and communities that spread across China. Their work was far beyond any job description which man might design.

Though many of these men and women did move to different parts of the world, and worked tirelessly in new fields of ministry, the perfume of their intercessory prayer continued to pervade the landscape they had left behind. Today, some of them are returning to visit their beloved China, and to meet with those who can testify to the "special power that seemed to come from somewhere." The "power" that gave them the strength they needed not only to survive, but to grow.

It may be a long time before we again witness such a glorious chapter in Church history which so graphically testifies to the beauty of the bonds of love that are woven by the tear-drenched fiber of intercessory prayer.

2. *Radio.* During some of the darkest days of the post-Cultural Revolution period (1969–1970), there was an international conference on communications. Some of the most respected leaders in Christian communications and the communication revolution were meeting. At that gathering, the person responsible for the direction of twenty hours per day of broadcasting to the People's Republic of China was severely chastised by several of the communications experts for "wasting money and time" broadcasting to China. He was told, "They have no radios and besides, they are all Communists. They won't listen, even if they could."

Dr. Robert Bowman, President of Far East Broadcasting Company, the organization doing the broadcasting, simply told his program director: "The radios are there, the people are there, the transmitters are there, the preachers are preaching, the burden and vision are there. You carry on your responsibilities and let me take care of the critics."

This story is not meant to belittle anyone, but rather to point out that God's ways are not always man's ways, and perhaps we could say that where there is no vision, expertise faileth.

Now, twenty years later, we see how right Dr. Bowman was. The renowned expert in church growth, Dr. Donald McGavran, wrote to Dr. Bowman after a recent trip to China and said, "What has happened seems to be that, facing the empty promises of Communism and the terrific opposition of the Cultural Revolution, many, many millions of Chinese have embraced

Christianity. Since they could not have a Bible, they copied various books [of the Bible] by hand and passed them around, and in many other ways have embraced the Christian faith."

Dr. McGavran continues: "Some communities are entirely Christian; some fifty percent and some ten percent. Christian broadcasts into China have beyond question furnished a major part of the motivation for this great movement, and the entire missionary work is deeply indebted to you."[1]

In the terrible days of persecution and feelings of abandonment, the "heavens [were] telling of God and His glory." Believers in China now report how important radio was to them: "You fed us who had no spiritual food from any other source." Another wrote: "You gave us the only Bible we had." (The Bible was read at dictation speed over the radio and one can still find copies of the handwritten Scriptures.)

Others wrote: "You served as a continual reminder that we were not alone, that we were part of a larger Body, and that we were not forgotten"; "You supplied an alternative for those who could no longer accept the continuous barrage of Maoist-Marxist doctrine that was keeping the country in a continual state of slavery."

Recently, a foreign tourist in China was approached by a young Chinese. After a brief conversation, the young man told of listening to Christian radio and what an effect it has had on his entire family. Due to restrictions, the conversation ended as abruptly as it began. However, the next morning, when the tourist was getting on the bus, a hand reached out and passed him a paper napkin. Written on the napkin was the FEBC broadcast schedule to China with program names, times, and frequencies. The young man wanted the American to know that he meant what he said about the radio broadcasts.

The part that radio played in the building of the Body of believers in China may be best illustrated by the words of a hymn that was the first song ever broadcast on the FEBC transmitter in Manila, transmitters that would later, and for three decades, broadcast the gospel to a land where ". . . we would

[1]Personal correspondence of October 28, 1983. Used with permission.

crawl under a blanket in our home, all of us, and listen to the radio from Manila." It was their church, and the hymn sung was "All Hail the Power of Jesus' Name," verse three:

"Let every kindred, every tribe,
On this terrestrial ball,
To Him all majesty ascribe,
And crown Him Lord of all."[2]

3. *Doing it right the first time.* Much negative material has been printed about the missionary activity in China through Hudson Taylor to 1949. What again is ignored in all of this is a very simple fact. If you take a map of the areas where the house church is, as Dr. McGavran says, "communities . . . some entirely Christian, some fifty percent and some ten percent Christian," and overlay it on an earlier map on China, indicating where there was a strong evangelical missionary movement prior to 1949, you will see the two merge and become one.

One cannot help but credit the early missionaries who though not perfect (none of us are) were overtly dedicated to message first and methodology second. Those early missionaries seemed to understand the concept that Jesus Christ said He would bless His Word, but the promise did not necessarily extend beyond that. The Word was primary; the method, though important, was negotiable.

Their generation might best be expressed in a eulogy recently given at the funeral of one who lived out this thesis. He was a man of great spiritual insight, intellectual perception, and who believed in the use of modern technology to preach the gospel. It was an area in which he was a pioneer, and whose influence will be felt for years: "Dr. Eugene Bertermann was no technical freak, but rather a man with a tremendous passion for the souls of man." Fortunately for China, message over methodology was lived out by the early missionaries as well as the Dr. Bertermanns, and practiced with great benefit to the gospel by the house church in China today.

4. *The supreme sacrifice.* When the history books are written, one fact must stand out above all others: There would not

[2]*Hymns for the Family of God* (Nashville: Paragon), p. 325.

be the church in China today had it not been for those believers who were *willing to pay the price*. They are the uncounted thousands of men and women of every age, who "counted it all joy" to die for the sake of the gospel of Jesus Christ.

Though they locked them in prison, tore families apart, burned their Bibles, closed their churches, those who survived still continued to preach. Rarely will you find a believer in China today who will even consider that the cost is too high. Many still carry physical scars which some call their "birthmarks into the Kingdom."

Their testimonies, which often must be practically pulled from them, in that they figure suffering is just part of being a Christian, reveal to all who will listen a glorious chapter of joy and sorrow, peace and, for some, disquiet.

Read these brief testimonies and you will agree. They all teach a special lesson for believers anywhere in the world.

"There were twenty-two people in our cell. We had twelve minutes to go to the bathroom. Anything not done in those few minutes had to be done in the cell. Some were 'reeducated,' but no one was released until all were 'reeducated.' To be the last of the twenty-two to betray our Lord made life very difficult."

"We would pray, sing to ourselves, and write sermons in our minds to keep our minds clear. Those who did not know Scripture had a very bad time. Those who could not repeat Scripture back to the Lord often either betrayed the Master and us, went insane, and/or committed suicide. It was the Word of God that kept us from doing any of the three."

"We not only survived . . . but look at us—we grew!"

"The more difficult things became, the more we seemed to grow. For a time we had a tendency to mix Marxism and Christianity. When they burned our Bibles, threw us out of our churches, sent our pastors away, we realized the two did not mix."

"We never met for any other reason than to pray, sing, and study our little pieces of Scripture. We often did not even ask for any of the latest news; we did not want to waste time. We were meeting illegally, and worshiping the Lord was the only thing we had in life worth getting caught doing."

"We prayed for our leaders and those who persecuted us. We saw many of our enemies become our friends, and some became brothers and sisters."

The question was asked of one lady: "Would you do it over again?"

"Do it over" to her would mean separation from her family, while spending eighteen years in prison, with all the physical, mental and spiritual battles inherent in such a life.

She first looked at me as though to say, "I'm surprised you have to ask such a question," and then with a broad smile, lifting her face, she replied, "Would I do it over again? I wouldn't want to miss the Lord's will. It was like eighteen years of Bible school!"

The tuition was a bit more than most of us would be willing to pay, but one look at her illuminated face testified to the outstanding curriculum.

Intercessory prayer, radio, planting of the seed, willingness to pay the price are all exciting chapters in how the church in China not only survived, but is still growing today.

Chapter Eight

Are There Missionaries in China's Future?

To be more specific: Will the Westerner, or non-Chinese, ever be able to return to China as a missionary?

The answer: "Yes, but . . ."

First, we have to realize that the believer in China may have a more important role as a missionary to the West than we would have to them. However, this does not negate the fact that there are some real weaknesses in the church in China today which could be strengthened by "outsiders."[1]

Basically, two questions must be asked: (1) Who are the people to be reached? and (2) What kind of person can reach them; that is, what are the missionary qualifications?

First, of the people of China, who are the ones reached?

Let's look at just one segment of China's society. Of the more than one billion people in China today, half are under the age of 20, of which 200 million are teenagers; 65 percent are under 30, that is 650 million people. These have all been born since "liberation." They are supposed to be ideologically pure, with all traces of capitalism and other concepts of "foreign substances" removed.

They represent an entire generation of birthright Marxists-Maoists freed from the "barbaric influence" of the "Western world."

---

[1]The house church is very anxious to receive Bible teachers from outside China. They realize the need for foundational teaching of God's Word.

They have gone through the educational process of the school of reality, and have been taught the finer points of Marxism-Maoism since they could first think or speak. One would think that they would be more Marxist than Mao himself; that they would be purer than the "new water of the Yangtze," and redder than the sun setting over Mao's tomb at the far end of Heavenly Square.

They aren't.

The government of Beijing realizes the tremendous problem that a geriatric leadership faces in "bringing the masses," that is, the young people, "into line."

The People's Daily, the official organ of the party in Beijing, echoes that concern with these disquieting words:

"After ten years of turmoil, many young people find their old political and moral beliefs shattered with new concepts yet to take place. As a result, they feel empty spiritually and they are in misery."

A young Chinese puts it much more succinctly:

"I've never lived a good day in my life. My mother was beaten to death, my father was left senseless, and I will have to beg for everything. This is what the Cultural Revolution did. It is unfixable. My scars will never heal."[2]

Basically, the young people can be broken down into two groups: (1) the "little soldiers of the Cultural Revolution," who are no longer "little" or "soldiers"; and (2) those who have been born since 1968, or were too young to participate in the Cultural Revolution.

Those "little soldiers" who have since burned both their arm bands and little red book are often referred to as the "lost generation." They are caught between the teenagers and those forty and above. It was this group of Red Guard members who, while in their late teens, were taught that it was a virtue to humiliate and persecute anyone over thirty. Many of those "over thirty" that were sent to reeducation camps, whose homes and lives were temporarily destroyed by the marauding youth, are today in positions of authority, and are not sympathetic to those who

---

[2]Fox Butterfield, *China: Alive on the Bitter Sea* (NYT Books, 1982), p. 126.

"put us in the cow pen and forced us to do menial work."

The vast majority of this "lost generation" have no education. They themselves closed down the schools for almost a decade, burning the books and sending professors to labor camps.

Added to this are today's teenagers who look with disdain at the Cultural Revolution and are out of sympathy with their elder brothers and sisters who disrupted the education system and nearly destroyed the country. Many of today's teenagers stood by as little children and watched the zealots of Mao burn their homes and persecute their parents. They have not forgotten.

So, today, the former Red Guard—the young people of the sixties—are caught between the old and the young . . . a lost generation with no education, too young to be retired, affected by cynicism, disillusioned and for many just below the surface, a hate waiting to be unleashed.

Merge these millions with those in their teens and middle twenties and you have over a half billion people, ranging from 18 to 35, who are, in their own words, "alienated, cynical and redundant."

A report by a Harvard University sociologist who spent a year in China amplified not only the problem the leadership faces in China but the opportunities we face.

"The young person," says Dr. Thomas Gold, "unchallenged by his job, spends most of his time either gossiping about which cadre is sleeping with which female employee, or trying to exchange cassette tapes out on the street."

He found three types of young people in Chinese cities:

1. The former Red Guard, the "lost generation" of Chairman Mao's Cultural Revolution of the 1960s. He calls them a "threat to stability and a potential obstacle to modernization—experienced at using disruption to gain attention, with some of them continuing open political activity and even violence."

2. Teenagers born during the Cultural Revolution whose education was disrupted by it, and who "seem to lack a social conscience or sense of higher purpose. Many feel politics is dangerous and concentrate on schoolwork, but others turn to crime, causing people in the cities to be afraid to go out alone at night."

3. The group in the middle is described by Dr. Gold as "hav-

ing a stronger basic education and moral training, but just as good at protesting as the former Red Guard." They are not yet the lost generation, says Gold, but "the government performance will dictate their loyalty."[3]

A similar assessment was published in *Newsweek* magazine. "Yang Ming is a twenty-year-old high school graduate with a passion for motorbikes. But since he has no job and no money to buy a bike, he steals them for joy rides around Shanghai. Lu Wei, nineteen, wanted to go live in the United States, but her hopes quickly vanished when a relative living in America balked at acting as her sponsor. Now she seethes with frustration. 'I don't really believe in Marxism or any religion,' she snarls. 'I only believe in good public relations. That's the secret to moving ahead here.'

"Their clothes, their manners, and their goals mark a surprisingly large number of the youth of Shanghai as a different breed in today's China. Young men and women wear body-hugging shirts in loud colors and with garish designs, bell-bottom trousers and stylish sunglasses. Many make a point of dining out on Western food, even though they usually have trouble with their knives and forks. Naturally, thousands of Shanghai youth do not fit this new mold, clinging instead to the dress styles and party-line attitudes of generations past. However, countless others are indeed a 'new generation—fun-loving and politically blasé, brash, and cynical.

"Perhaps their cynicism is understandable. Not long ago their counterparts were the spearhead of the Cultural Revolution—mobilized by Mao Tse-tung to cleanse China of its wayward, bourgeois ways. Millions of Shanghai's youth were recruited by Mao and later by the Shanghai-based Gang of Four—in the zealous campaign against capitalism and pragmatism. Now, history has consigned the Cultural Revolution to the dustbin, leaving the current generation uncertain about their future. 'We are a redundant generation, we know that,' said one unemployed twenty-year-old. 'There's not much room for us in society, so we don't aim for anything high. "Be practical" has become our slogan.'

---

[3]*South China Morning Post*, Hong Kong, April 16, 1981, p. 3.

"Some of the rebellious youth are college students. Others work in factories or on state farms. Many are unemployed. But they share a common complaint: the Chinese Communist Party, in their view, has failed the people. Some of them have embraced capitalism, the route they think will lead to good food, flashy cars, comfortable homes and easy and well-paying jobs. 'The young people here are sleek and selfish and think only of consumer goods,' said an American who lives in Shanghai.

"Because they see their lives as bereft of meaning and direction, Shanghai's youth have embraced a self-serving philosophy. 'It's not enough to get a job, earn money, find a nice friend and enjoy a soft life,' says one teenager. 'We've had enough of those slogans.' The city's youth seem materialistic even when it comes to marriage. 'Our ideal partners are not necessarily the brains-and-beauty type,' one young woman confided. 'Rather, they must come from a family with some money. Most important, they must have a spacious apartment.'

"High on the list of 'necessities' for young people in Shanghai is a motorbike—the latest status symbol in China. Yang Ming and his friends discovered that they could open the lock on a bike with a chopstick. After stealing five bikes, Yang Ming was caught, clapped into jail and fined $40. But thanks to his father, a middle-ranking party member, Yang Ming was set free after serving a two-week sentence and his fine was waived.

"Such petty crimes are now common among young people in Shanghai, but there are those who have not joined the rebels. A small minority still cling to conventional ideals, though the emphasis now is more on patriotism than Maoism. They want to see China 'rich and strong,' as one puts it. They say they want to preserve the present social system, but with reforms that include more liberal policies on personal matters. And they see no reason why their country, with its rich civilization and immense resources, should continue to be the 'sick old maid' of Asia after thirty years of Communism. They may be lone voices, but for China's current leadership, they represent a ray of hope amid a sea of youthful cynicism and despair."[4]

---

[4]*Newsweek*, August 17, 1981.

What can the 650 million young people of China look forward to?

How about advanced education? 210 million students are of school age, but 50 percent of these will find no room in high school. Of the 50 percent that do complete high school, only 3 percent will go on to college. Most of them will be the favored "sons of the Revolution," that is, cadre leaders and children of the officers of the People's Liberation Army.

The *People's Daily* reports: "The vast majority banned from college doors are left in the cold, bewildered and despaired about the future. How can they expect to find socialism attractive and not suffer from ideological confusion?"

Marriage?

Men are to be twenty-seven; girls at least twenty-two. The chances are slim to zero that they will have a home of their own. Houses are just not available. They will be strongly "encouraged" to have only one child. The "encouragement" is actually a state policy on birth control. It is not optional as these recent reports from Chinese newspapers indicate.

—A commune worker was recently expelled from the Communist Party after she gave birth to her fourth child. She said she would rather lose party membership than not have a son.

—A warning from officials that couples who violate China's one-child birth control policy face the loss of more than fifteen percent of their pay under new regulations announced in Shanxi Province.

—A woman Communist party member who violated China's "one-child-per-family" policy has been put on one year's party probation.

The "encouragements" are backed up by Article 49 of the Constitution which interpreted by the Beijing press reads: "There is a financial penalty that should be imposed on a couple who fail to carry out family planning by having more than one child. A second baby is not to be allowed except in special circumstances, and subsequent births are to be banned altogether." This is a quote from a directive issued by the party's central committee and the state council, and to disobey is to be counterrevolutionary.

In China, the greatest possession is not just a child, but a male child. He is not only the preserver of the family line, but also social security. What do they do with the girls when families are allowed only one child?

This report from *Newsweek* magazine, February 21, 1983, gives some indication. "On a cold night in Shandong Province last December, Liu Shunsan, an illiterate peasant, threw his four-year-old daughter down a well. According to the *China Youth News*, he ignored her cries of 'Papa, Papa.' He calmly 'lit a cigarette and peered into the well until he was sure that she was really dead.' Liu had what he thought was good reason to kill his only child: his wife was again pregnant and this time a local fortune-teller assured him 'it would be a son.' Rather than risk having an abortion, ordered by local family-planning officials seeking to enforce one-child-per-family rules, he took what he saw as the only course to ensure himself an heir. 'Without a son, the generations cannot be passed on,' he told a court that early this month sentenced him to 15 years in prison. Today, Liu is still without a son. The child that was born shortly after the murder turned out to be another girl.

"Gruesome accounts of young girls drowned in rivers, suffocated in their sleep or simply abandoned in the fields have become a regular event in the Chinese press. They are part of an official crusade against the resurgence of one of China's oldest social vices, female infanticide. Pressed by the rigorous birth-control regulations, parents have reportedly mutilated baby girls to take advantage of loopholes allowing a second child if the first is born deformed. They have resorted to another ancient practice—the buying and selling of children—either to bachelors unable to find brides, or to couples who are childless. There have been numerous reports of wives being harassed or killed by husbands enraged by their failure to produce a son to carry on the family name.

"Slogans such as 'These are different times; boys and girls are equal' are being given heavy publicity in an effort to override time-worn proverbs such as 'A boy can shoulder the roof beam, while a girl cannot even prop up a door frame.' There have also been educational displays, particularly in the countryside, showing that a man's sperm ultimately determines a child's sex. The campaign is more than simply moral or academic; according to a recent study, by the year 2010 China will have 169 males of marriageable age for every 100 females, if the current one-child-only policy continues. The social problems from that sort of imbalance as much as population growth are beginning to worry Chinese planners."

It is not just the Western press that is documenting a crime that reeks of a combination of Herod, Hitler, and Stalin.

Articles collected from the Chinese press itself fortify the evidence of a tragedy of uncalculated shame in the making.

—"Two women committed suicide in the city of Shenyang after their husbands tormented them for giving birth to baby girls. Twenty such cases happened in that northeastern city in 1982."

—"More and more Chinese hospitals are now able to test the sex of unborn babies. More and more people are taking advantage of it to have an abortion in case the test reveals a baby girl."

—"A father maimed his daughter of eight months by biting off part of her nose. This entitles him to have a second child, hopefully a boy."

—"Wan Chuwen, a 26-year-old worker from Dandong City in Lianoning Province, has been convicted of killing his baby daughter for reasons of 'social importance.' It stems from the lingering feudal idea which places men above women and sons above daughters."

—"A father who wanted a son instead of a daughter has been jailed for 13 years for smothering his two-month-old daughter and tossing her body down a well."

—"The most vicious punishment mentioned so far is the attempted electrocution of a young woman in northern China. To punish her for having a girl, her husband diverted an electric current to the handle of their apartment door."

It is generally admitted that the next three years are crucial to China's population policy if she is to keep her population below 1.2 billion by the end of the century. During these three years, 78 million young Chinese—the number amounts to the combined populations of East and West Germany—will get married and start families.

Some Chinese are alarmed at the fact that abortions have become too common in Beijing. Officials say, "They should not be regarded as a normal method of birth control." According to a survey of more than 15,000 abortions, 40 percent were performed on women who had had one previously, and some women had had seven or eight in all. A high proportion was performed on women who had become pregnant again soon after birth which, the paper said, was due to the popular myth that contraception was not necessary during that time.

At the end of the year, a special conference organized by the Ministry of Health decided that: "It should be easier for unmarried women to get abortions. They should not be degraded, criticized or reported to their employer or other authorities. The rate of abortions performed on unmarried women accounts for as much as seventy percent of all abortions in some urban areas, such as Beijing and Shanghai. Teenage girls who engage in premarital sex are sometimes considered delinquent and sent to special schools or reeducation farms . . . some women have been so distraught at their treatment in state clinics that they have threatened suicide. They sometimes seek out illegal abortionists or ask friendly doctors to quietly arrange an abortion through 'kuanxi,' or backdoor connections, with no questions asked."

The ugliness of every abortion is perhaps only surpassed by female infanticide.

Fifteen peasant women from a small village in central China, in defiance of Beijing's strict population control policies, have publicly declared they would rather die than give up their chance of a baby boy.

The fifteen women from a village in Anhui Province said that, as mothers of girls, "they lacked status and were targets of mistreatment by their husbands, mother-in-law and even their own parents." The Chinese press is full of similar stories. Officials admit that their population control is doomed as long as men are considered superior to women.

The facts which follow represent an unmitigated horror story:

1. Faced with massive resistance to its one-child policy, particularly in Guangdong Province with a population of more than 59 million, the provincial government broadcasted an order over Radio Canton on May 14 to the effect that women pregnant with their second child must undergo abortions.

2. Also in Guangdong, two women were locked up for 15 days as "sorceresses" for inciting pregnant women to flee from family-planning workers. All but 9 of the 325 women with unauthorized pregnancies were later given abortions.

3. In some villages, a bucket of water is readied by the bedside of the mother-to-be. If the child is a girl, she is immediately drowned. Other parents dump unwanted infants in caves, fields or on mountainsides, strangle them, poison them or throw them into public toilets.

One final example of government policy on birth control is as follows: This is a story published by the *People's Daily*, China's official newspaper, titled "Current Information." The article tells of an incident in Henan Province in which the country party authorities had been lax in implementing the government birth-control campaign. When the local cadres realized there were 3,000 more women pregnant than their quota for the year permitted, they suddenly ordered a "clean out the stomachs" movement. All 3,000 women were ordered to undergo immediate abortions, including one expectant mother almost nine months along. Some of the women fled into hiding; when the cadres came around to find them, children in the neighborhood organized themselves into an anti-government militia to warn the pregnant women and help them escape.

Concerning the choices that are available to young people in education, marriage, raising a family, and the other aspects of living that so many of us take for granted, it is easy to see why one of the most sought after books in China today is *Joni*, the story of a young quadraplegic. This book has been illegally translated and copies are made by hand, passed around and read one chapter at a time. The young people see in this young lady a parallel to their own predicament. They, too, are "crippled" (paralyzed) through a "terrible accident" (Communism). They are confined to a wheelchair (party leadership and the system). They are not free to stand or to walk. But in *Joni* "we see someone who has overcome all this pain and grief. We understand her."[5]

Who Is to Be Reached?

Basically we are talking about over a billion people, whose average age is 28. People who have never lived under any system but Communism, but who are now in rebellion against that system. Never mind what Mao did with them or Teng, or Hua, or even Hudson Taylor. They are now ours. What are we going to do with them?

"Alienated," "cynical," and "tired of slogans," but more than that, they are described by one official as "a slate wiped clean eagerly awaiting the presence of the first person who will come and write something meaningful."

The pen is in our hands!

Who Can Reach Them?

What kind of person qualifies to hold such a pen? How does one earn the privilege of writing the Name of Jesus Christ upon the slate "wiped clean"?

It might be well to review a little Chinese history for some clues.

There is the Great Wall. A fortification about 1500 miles long, stretching from the Gulf of Chihil of the Yellow Sea to the gate of Central Asia. It is the greatest building enterprise ever undertaken by man; the only object on earth that astronauts could identify. It was built three centuries before Christ, which was also before dirt movers, caterpillar tractors, and unions.

There is the Grand Canal, which runs for 1200 miles, built 589 years after Christ. Still no dirt movers, caterpillar tractors or unions. It was built by the sweat of the Chinese people. Both

---

[5]For an in-depth study of some of the daily problems faced by the Chinese, especially those in rural areas, one should read Steven Mosher's *Broken Earth: The Rural Chinese*, Free Press, 1983.

represent a nation that knows how to pay a price to accomplish a task.

More contemporary is the Long March. It is the cornerstone of Maoist mythology. In 1934, Mao and his Communist army was surrounded by the forces of Chiang Kai-shek. The Communists split into two forces and headed north to establish the Communist capital of Yenan, 6,000 miles away. There were no trains, no buses, and in many cases, no shoes. Six thousand miles through wild, mountainous swamps, snow, ice, and dirt. To add a little discouragement along the way, there were ten Nationalist armies stationed in the different provinces. Mao's forces crossed eighteen mountain ranges on foot, twenty-four rivers (without benefit of rafts), and fought at least one action every day. In one instance, they had to cross a 300-foot suspension bridge suspended on sixteen iron chairs. There were machine guns positioned on the far side to discourage their crossing. It was the only way to Yenan. Mao's troops slung their weapons on their back and hand-over-hand they went across the bridge. When one would fall into the river, a victim of machine gun fire, another would take his place. One finally made it across and grenaded the machine gun nest.

Another bridge was covered with paraffin and when Mao's troops started across, it was set afire. The troops put the fire out by running through the flames.

One hundred and thirty thousand began the march; twenty thousand arrived at the caves of Yenan.

Like Mao said, "Revolution is no dinner party." They were ready to suffer and die for their leader and their ideology. China understands that kind of a person.

Perhaps they are only events. What about men? In the end, history is changed not so much by marching armies as by one single man. One such person was a young Russian man by the name of Mikhail Gusenberg, later to become Michael Borodin.

He had been a schoolteacher in Indiana and Chicago. Later, he would become an underground courier to the United States for the party.

In 1923, Lenin sent him to China as an advisor to help reorganize the Kuomintang into a strong disciplined and centralized party. His disciples were Sun Yat-sen, Chiang Kai-shek, and a young Vietnamese by the name of Ho Chi Minh.

An American correspondent interviewed Borodin. The content should tell us more about the type of missionary that will have the necessary credentials to answer the call of the house church to "Come and help us."

"They say, Mr. Borodin, that you are here to take over China. I am sure my paper would be interested to know if this is true, or if not, just why you have come?"

"That's easy," he replied. "If you say my colleagues and I plan to take over this country, the anwer is no. But if you say we believe that our ideas will one day take it over, the answer is yes. China has suffered for hundreds of years. She wants help. She has asked us for it, and we intend to give it. That is why I am here. Have you any objections?"

"No," I countered with an effort at nonchalance. "But, do you have any notion of what you are taking on? I was born here and I know. How many people do you think live in this country?"

"About five hundred million. Why?"

"Don't tell me you seriously mean to take over a fifth of the human race. In the first place, you are too few. You're only a handful with no knowledge of the land or the language. You'll never do it in a thousand years."

"Oh yes, we will," came the cool reply. "You forget, young man, that I am not here for my health, or I would not be working in barbarous heat. I don't spend my time at the bars and races like the English and French. I am not interested in a career or a fortune like the Americans. I serve an ideology. And with an ideology, it is not numbers that count. It is dedication. You Americans would not understand that. I have lived many years in your country and I know what goes on. You concentrate on comfort and personal success. You had the chance. But you don't care. I'm interested in China. I am here to help her find something that will change things."

"Do you enjoy your work in China, Mr. Borodin?"

"Enjoy?" he echoed scornfully, "a bourgeois question. It is not a matter of whether we enjoy our work here. The work is necessary. That is all that counts. It is, of course, far from the friends, the concerts and the theater that mean so much in Moscow. But long ago I made up my mind that Communism alone held an answer for the world, because Communism, unlike modern religion, insists on changing things. And I decided I would go wherever I could help most. The party decided I could help most in China. Therefore, I was glad to come. Nothing else matters. Does that answer your question?"

After a long silence, Borodin began murmuring, half to himself, "You know," he mused, "I used to read the New Testament. Again and again I read it. It is the most wonderful story ever told. That man, Paul, he was a real revolutionary. I take my hat off to him." He made a symbolic gesture, his long black hair falling momentarily over his face.

Another long silence.

Then suddenly Borodin whirled around, his face contorted with fury as he shook his fist in my face.

"But where do you find him today?" he shouted. "Answer me that, Mr. Roots. Where do you find him? Where? Where? Where?"[6]

Michael Borodin died in obscurity under house arrest in the Soviet Union, a victim of Joseph Stalin's paranoia. But his question remains: "Where will we find men like Paul?"

Unfortunately Borodin never met Hudson Taylor, or Jonathan Goforth, or the hundreds of other young men and women who went to China because they, too, were sent as ambassadors, not for Lenin, but for Jesus Christ.

China understands men and women who are willing to build Great Walls, dig Grand Canals, die on Long Marches, disciple, live and die unknown, unheralded in a prison. That is the kind of person the Chinese will listen to.

The Tentmakers

Are there such people available today? Yes. One such group is called "tentmakers," some of whom are working in China

[6]Roots, John McComb, *Chou: An Informal Biography* (N.Y.: Doubleday, 1978), pp. 33–35.

today. These are the professional people who go to China as "foreign experts."

They are a very special kind of people with special qualifications—qualifications recently enunciated by one of the "experts" working in China, which give us a clearer definition of who they are.

1. A tentmaker must have spiritual preparation. There is no place for people depending on a regular church meeting for their spiritual food or fellowship. There will be no place for books, magazines, radio, tapes or television. Anyone feeling this kind of a call and who has the expertise needed by the Chinese government should begin to prepare before he arrives.

2. A tentmaker needs more than an average working knowledge of the Word of God and must be able to apply it without the use of a theological library, helps or aids.

3. A tentmaker should lead the kind of life that prays first and then acts. Prayer, for a tentmaker, is not a last resort.

4. A tentmaker should have experience in leading and interacting with small groups. He should have the desire to disciple as much as evangelize.

5. A tentmaker should have considerable exposure to international students before his assignment. He needs to know how other cultures think.

6. A tentmaker should spend some time in a Chinese church before going to China. He should eat in Chinese homes, live with a family for a period of time and absorb some of the aspects of a Chinese lifestyle.

7. Besides having Mandarin capability, or the ability to learn a difficult language, the tentmakers should study Christian apologetics—know why he believes what he does; he should have an understanding of Marxism, Leninism, Communist religious policies, Christianity and science, especially Darwinism; history of the Christian Church in China; the Three-Self church and the house church and its operation; and be able to answer such questions as why God allows suffering, etc.

8. A tentmaker must know what Chinese students study. If they speak English, they have probably learned it from such books as Sinclair Lewis and *Racial Prejudice in America*, Tol-

stoy and *Resurrection* and how it points out the evils of capitalism; Steinbecks' *Grapes of Wrath* and how desperate the situation is in America today.

9. A tentmaker must be a learner, willing to sit at the feet of others.

10. Perhaps most important, a tentmaker does not possess a "short-term mentality." It is not something he tries to experience to see if he likes it.

Does it work? Again, the answer is, "Yes, it does."

It is the "foreign expert" who, for the present at least, will be one of the witnesses. He is called, appropriately, "tentmaker."

Yes, but . . .

In answer to the question, *are there missionaries in China's future?* The answer remains, "Yes, but . . ."

We must understand whom we are to reach. Basically, we are talking about young people, who represent a major portion of the population.

We must be able to turn around the reasons why we lost China in the first place. We were out-witnessed, out-disciplined, and out-motivated. It is a process that we must now take in hand and reverse. It is now our turn to out-witness, out-discipline and out-motivate.

The pen is in our hand, the slate is clean, ready for the message, but before we apply the point to the surface, maybe we should think about a poem that another man wrote as the Communists were taking over Shanghai.

Tonight Shanghai is burning,
　　And I am dying, too.
But there is no death more certain,
　　Than death inside of you.
Some men die of shrapnel,
　　Some go down in flames
But most men die, inch by inch,
　　While playing little games.
—Source Unknown

Chapter Nine

Lessons Learned

It would be a tragedy if we simply read about the church in China and then failed to apply those lessons to our own lives, to our own fellowship of believers, to our own communities.

That is why it is so important to stop and listen to the message from the arena and then ask ourselves: "What are the lessons that we can learn from what has happened in China during the past decades?"

The lessons are many; but a few stand out as a primer for further study.

Things Not Transferable

In discussions about the church in China, one of the first responses is either, "That could never happen here," or "Let's make it happen in our country." Either response is a warning to take a closer look at what really did happen in China, and realize that the Lord does not always do things the same way twice. Though His principles never change, the effecting of those principles in the lives of people does change.

The first thing that is different in China from, say the United States, Canada, or other countries that are predominately capitalistic, is that the battle in China is rather easily defined. The purifying agents used in China was/is Marxism/Maoism/Leninism. Maoism is a synthetic form of Marxism, an economic policy devised of state ownership, combined with the revolutionary anarchy of Lenin.

Marxism/Leninism is basically a perversion of Christianity. Hence, the point of tension in China is rather easy to define. It is the person of Jesus Christ, *true* Christianity, versus Maoism/Marxism/Leninism, the *perversion* of Christianity. Spreading the gospel in China in the face of this perversion cannot be transferred to so-called Christian lands. There the problem and the perversion are entirely different.

The problem in the West is an erosion of biblical authority leading to the belief that man, not God, is the ultimate authority in the universe. This perversion of essential Christianity is the great problem in the West.

The great battle in the West is not the person of Jesus Christ (true Christianity) versus Marxism (a perversion of Christianity); rather, we have the person of Jesus Christ (true Christianity) versus materialism.

We can see that to try to transfer what has happened in China to the West, we must first of all admit that our greatest threat is not Marxism. It is materialism. Some might define this as materialistic capitalism. Granted, the battle will be decided in first cleaning up our own perversion before we take on another.

Another point should be made here, and that is related to the question, "Do we all have to undergo the persecution imposed by a Marxism regime?"

The answer is no, at least not in the same form. There are two reasons for this.

First, persecution comes basically in two forms: physical and mental. Perhaps we are under greater persecution today in the developed countries than we realize. The persecution is not physical, but rather mental. Take a look around you today and ask the question, "How many happy Christians do I really know in America, or Canada, or other Western countries?" The Christians of China, pre- and post-persecution, might give us a better definition of "joyful" than we could muster, where we enjoy all the supposed freedoms, while failing to realize that we are in effect prisoners of technology designed to perpetuate materialism.

Second, as one house church member pointed out, "If every country was like China, who would plant the seed? Our country is in the midst of a revival today because a country where you have great freedom sent men and women to plant the seed. Had that seed not been planted, we would not have a revival in China today."

It is dangerous to dictate to the Lord how He should accomplish His task. His ways are not only beyond understanding, but are as different as each of His creatures.

God Uses the Wrath of Man to Praise Him

We got our first hint of this in 1980, when the prestigious *Far East Economic Review* (Aug. 15, 1980) did a cover story entitled "Back to the Basics." It dealt with the revival of religion in China, and in one section headed "Checking the Fervor of Born-Again Christians," it stated, ". . . That drive to wipe out religion in China failed. Catholics and Protestants both maintain that today's devotees are more enthusiastic than ever. . . . Recently a reader's letter in the *China Youth News* exhorted young people to 'understand that religion is opium for lulling the people.' "

Meanwhile, the *People's Liberation Daily* also criticized soldiers who dared to pursue ". . . anarchy and ultraindividualism—and even go so far as to believe in Christ for spiritual solace."

The article (in the FEER) then went on to explain the effect that the early missionaries had on this "born-again" revival in China:

"At the same time, a little-recognized phenomenon in Chinese Marxism has been of considerable importance to the development of China's post-revolutionary society. That is the influence of missionary Christianity in shaping some of the fundamental assumptions of Mao and other historic leaders. Neither Mao nor any of the other famous Chinese revolutionaries were mission-educated, but in the condition of early twentieth-century China, it was impossible for a young man or woman to seek knowledge and ideas about the modern world without unconsciously absorbing some of the basic concepts of Christianity. The missions were instrumental in bringing many Western ideas and organizations to China—the YMCA, theological seminaries, Western medicine, organized sports, knowledge of Western music, languages and literature—all of them tightly bound up with the Western concept of civilization based on Christian belief."

The article continues, "Some basic ideas and practices of the Chinese Communists, especially under Mao, show a correspondence with Christian principle which is hard to write off as coincidence.

"The importance of confession, self-examination, honesty before one's god/party, compassion, ideological rectitude . . ." is necessary.

Some of these traits did not exist to any degree until Mao enforced them. It is something that might have taken several generations of missionaries to do.

Mao, also by his leadership, created in China the best possible climate in which to influence people; for example, painful uneasiness or anxiety; feeling of separation from a group, or the rest of the world; feeling of pointlessness, that there is really no future, so why bother, let's either burn the place down or leave.

Imagine, if you will, a young person who is "cynical, alienated and distrustful" of Maoism. A person who understands the importance of confession, self-examination, honesty before one's God or god, compassion and ideological purity. Give that person the right message—to put into that vacuum chisled there by Mao—the message of the Person of Jesus Christ, and you can see part of the *why* of the revival. Mao, though he did not plan it that way, did a good job of preparing the most populated nation in the world to receive the gospel of Jesus Christ.

But that is not all. Veteran missionary Paul Kauffman tells of his father who went to Tibet in 1907. From the end of the last public transportation, the trip required 40 days by mule. Many missionaries never completed the rough journey. They died and their mules went on alone. Thanks to Mao, there is now the famous Qinghag-Tibet line, the first railway to penetrate Tibet, and you can ride in either a soft-seated car or a sleeper. In 1949, there were about 75,000 kilometers of serviceable roads in China. Today, there are over 890,000 kilometers of roads for transportation.

Thanks to Mao, the country is wired for radio.

In 1949, China had 300 main languages and many minor dialects. Today, thanks to Mao, there is one major language: Mandarin.

What the Romans and Greeks did for the New Testament church, Mao did for the twentieth-century church in China.

There are few illustrations in the world today as vivid as China in explaining the fact that "surely the wrath of men shall praise *You*" (Ps. 76:10, NKJV).

The Messiah Complex

Robert Lifton, in his book on Mao and the Cultural Revolution,[1] points out that ". . . the activist response to symbolic death—or to what might be called unmastered death anxiety—is a quest for rebirth."

The Cultural Revolution was Mao's bid for "rebirth" for "immortality." He had his Bible—the "little red book." He had people bowing and giving thanks before meals for their "great leader's provision." His speeches were laced with words like "demons, devils," and he was vying against supernatural enemies. He saw himself as master of the universe.

This is always the danger when a man who is used to having absolute power begins to lose some of that control through the natural aging process. When a man places himself above all others, he begins to actually believe that he is "immortal." He doesn't want to die, but if he should, he wants to leave something that will be immortal, a memorial to his greatness. The last thing he wants is to be forgotten.

Then, when the day comes that he begins to lose the grasp he once had; when he sees that people are beginning to turn to others for leadership; and he wonders if he might not be im-

[1]Robert Lifton, *Revolutionary Immortality* (London: Penguin, 1970), p. 22.

mortal after all, he is apt to do something very ridiculous, like starting a Cultural Revolution.

It is a lesson worth learning. We all need someone to whom we can be responsible, or accountable. We all need to realize our fragility, the shortness of life. We all need to realize that our memorial is something we send on before, not something we leave behind. We all have to give up the helm at some time. When we reach that point and we fail to grasp our immortality, there is a tendency to do some very foolish things in order to regain the influence we once had.

Perhaps one of the blessings for China is that Mao's children died violent deaths while serving the party, helping to make the "old man" immortal. Consequently, when Mao died, there was not an heir apparent to be thrust upon the people to carry on the sham of "immortality."

If there are to be any memorials, let others build them after we are gone, so that we will have nothing to say about them and would be embarrassed if we knew they existed.

The Messiah Complex can be a deadly disease that is not limited to the People's Republic of China, or even to that system which is a perversion of Christianity.

A Lesson on Being a Pilgrim

It is possible to be an Old Testament pilgrim in a twentieth-century world.

The believers in China seem to understand that when Adam and Eve sinned, they were evicted from their home, the Garden of Eden. Jesus said that He was going to build a new home for them but in the meantime, we are pilgrims between two events.

The believers in China are much like Abraham who left the splendor of Ur to walk in faith as a pilgrim. The Chinese Christians may not have much of a home now, but there is little doubt that they look forward expectantly to the splendor of that new home that has been promised them at the feet of their Lord. They seem to realize that this life is a bridge and though we walk over bridges, we are not to build homes on them. As one put it: "We pilgrims carry small backpacks."

How to be an Old Testament pilgrim in a twentieth-century world is a lesson we could all learn. China has given us an example worth following.

Lessons on Forgiveness

Much Scripture is devoted to the matter of a loving and forgiving God. Forgiveness is the visible attribute of love, and how visible it is in the house church in China.

During the early days of the Cultural Revolution, the Red Guards dragged away a husband and a father, leaving behind a wife and a son. Later they would kill the son, and the father would die in prison.

Some years later that young Red Guard, now a cadre, who was responsible for the death of the father and son, had a son of his own, an only son. One must remember how important a son is in today's society in China—not only the importance of an heir, but also in light of the one-child-per-family policy.

This lady, whose husband and only son had been killed under the direction of the cadre, heard that his only son was critically ill. She had some experience in nursing people back to health. She went to the cadre's house with her meager supply of medicine, but a heart full of forgiveness. For three nights and two days she sat at the bedside of that son, whose father had dealt such devastation to her family, and nursed him back to health. There was no hate; she did it because "that is what Christ did for me." (This actual event illustrates what has happened again and again all across China.) How many problems in this world would be solved today if we learned well this lesson of forgiveness.

What a fulfillment this is of Proverbs 25:21, 22: "If your enemy is hungry, give him bread to eat. If he is thirsty, give him water to drink, for you shall heap coals of fire on his head."

I always liked the part of "heaping coals of fire on his head." That sounded like revenge to me—sanctified revenge. Actually, it means something quite different. In Old Testament times, the people were often nomadic. They had no matches. One of their most valued possessions were hot coals that they put in a round container and carried to the place where they would encamp. It was the ladies' job to carry these coals and to make sure the food was cooked. Without fire, they could go hungry. This cylindrical container of hot coals was one of the most important possessions of any group of people, and when they met strangers or enemies along the way, God said they were to share those coals so that others could eat as well. They were to share their most precious possession with those who would spitefully use them.

What a living illustration we have of this, not only in this one lady who nursed back to health the son of the man who murdered her husband and son, but of thousands of other believers in China as well. This is a lesson that is going to take some application before we really understand it.

Another lesson is the importance of the *Word*. The *Word* hidden in the heart is the one thing that keeps one from sinning against Him. Time and time again, Chinese believers testified as to how those who had memorized much Scripture, and during the times of persecution would rest on that Word. One reported: "Those who have a good knowlege of the Word of God and could repeat it back to the Lord during the difficult times survived even the most terrible persecution. Inevitably those who had little knowledge of His Word would give up their faith, and in many cases commit suicide."

A Final Testimony

Perhaps all of these lessons are best summarized in an interview with a Christian in China who spent twenty-three years and ten months in prison because of his faith in Jesus Christ. He called it "a great university where he learned many, many great lessons."[2]

---

[2]As I have already said, the Christians in China who went behind the bamboo curtain in 1948 included the whole range of believers. Some were very good, some good, some ordinary, and some very poor Christians. When the very good suffered intense persecution, their lives and witness proved wonderfully contagious.

This interview is an example of the latter. It was given in Shanghai to several foreign guests and is available in its complete context in English.

Q: Many Christians in the West find forgiveness a serious problem. How do we forgive when we have not even suffered? How are you able to forgive?

A: I don't remember any of the faults of those who have offended me. I can thoroughly forgive them. Because Jesus told us if you will forgive those who trespass against you, your Father in heaven will also forgive your trespasses; if you do not forgive others, our Father in heaven will not forgive you. Therefore, we should not hate anybody. Anyone who has hurt me, I am able to forgive them. This should be so, because I am a great sinner myself. If God has forgiven me, can I not forgive others?

Q: Did you have any Bibles in prison that you could read?

A: No, not a single Bible in the twenty-three years and ten months that I was there. I never saw a Bible even once during my imprisonment.

Q: Did you memorize the Bible?

A: Yes, I memorized many passages from the Scripture. I would not consider myself as one who knew his Bible well. I have trained myself to memorize Scriptures in long passages consisting of many verses, which I could readily recall during my imprisonment. Thus it did not matter that much whether I had a Bible with me or not. Even though I did not have any Bible, I had the Bible in my head, and so it was as though I had a Bible with me during my imprisonment. Of course, it was not as good as having a Bible before me to be able to read every detail of the Scriptures. But I remembered the important teaching and promises in the Scripture and I could dwell on them often. Thus, to have a Bible or not to have a Bible did not differ that much with me at that time. I was also able to memorize many hymns, both English and Chinese, although I could not remember the entire hymn—usually one or two verses. For I never dreamed of spending such a long period of my time in prison. If I had known that, I would have memorized many, many more Bible passages and hymns.

Q: Did you sing hymns while in prison?

A: Yes, but I would only sing in a low voice, alone, not wanting to disturb others. I would walk around the courtyard and sing in a low voice to myself.

He then sang two of his favorite hymns which he sang in prison, "Safe in the Arms of Jesus" and "All the Way My Savior Leads Me.")[3]

Q: What has kept your faith going all these years? Are there special verses which kept your faith strong as the days went by?

A: There are many passages from Scripture which helped me. Actually I can recite many passages from Scripture.

Q: What are the special verses that you like most?

A: A passage from Micah 7: "Therefore I will look unto the Lord; I will wait for the God of my salvation: my God will hear me. Rejoice not against me, O mine enemy: when I fall, I shall arise; when I sit in darkness, the Lord shall be a light unto me. I will bear the indignation of the Lord, because I have sinned against him, until he plead my cause, and execute judgment for me: he will bring me forth to the light, and I shall behold his righteousness. . . ."

Q: What was the most blessed time you had while you were in prison?

A: The more often I was tried and attacked, the more abundantly I received His grace. The words of Scripture became my strength after I had fallen; God through His Word enabled me to stand up again. Peter fell for one day only, but I fell for several years. Thanks be unto God, Peter was forgiven after he had bitterly cried in repentance. I did not shed tears, but in my heart there was severe pain. I confessed my sins and I repented and my Lord also forgave me. So like Peter, though I had failed miserably, yet I was able to rise up again. Peter's case gave me great comfort. It shows that, as a man falls, he comes to know his greatest weakness, and the Lord is able to change his weakness into strength. Paul said: "In my body there is a thorn; I prayed often to the Lord that He might cause the thorn to be

[3]Two things to keep in mind: (1) The Chinese educational system heavily emphasizes memorization. In that scriptural memorization cards, etc., were not available, many Chinese memorized large portions of Scripture; hence this man's testimony regarding memorization is fairly typical. (2) Next to the Bible, a hymnal is their most precious possession. This was true even before 1949. They worship with music in a way that is quite foreign to the "let's sing a song to get the people's attention" syndrome so prevalent in America.

removed from me, but the Lord said to me: 'My grace is sufficient for you, my strength is made manifest in your weakness.' I like to boast over my weakness, for it is in my weakness that I become strong." I have gone through a long period of failure, but thanks be unto God, from my failure I have turned to victory, even until now I can boast only in the Lord. Jeremiah said: "The wise should not boast over his wisdom, the rich should not boast over his riches, the warrior should not boast over his strength; he who boasts should boast because he knows that I am the Lord and knows that I perform justice and righteousness on the earth. Therefore I boast, says the Lord." Only after I had experienced severe failure, did I know how to trust my God. Therefore, today I can boast only in the Lord, not over how strong I am, but in that after I had fallen, the Lord enabled me to stand up again and made me become a strong man. I am now stronger than I was over twenty years ago.

Q: During all these years, did you have any word from other believers?

A: I did not receive any news, not a single letter from anyone except letters from my wife and son. But even they could not say much. Neither could I write much, and if I did, it would not be sent. So I was totally cut off from outside news.

Q: So the Lord allowed you to stay in prison as part of His will. He did not make a mistake, did He?

A: He did not make a single mistake. We know that "all things work for good to them that are called according to His will."

Q: If you had not been in prison, wouldn't you have done more work for the Lord?

A: No, the work that I did by staying in prison is greater than I could have done by not being in prison.

Q: Were you ever physically beaten while you were in prison?

A: I am sorry, I cannot talk about this. Here I don't want to let the world know about that aspect. God knows everything. Now since the government is turning toward the good, I will not mention anything of the past. I don't want the world to have a bad impression of our government. Since the government is turning to the good, who am I that I should recall past things?

We have the lessons. Will we now be worthy students?

Chapter Ten

The Future

Some Things That Haven't Changed

In its simplest terms, China remains a Marxist/Leninist nation. It is a highly controlled, totalitarian state. Any political changes we have seen over the past few years have been simply orchestrated undulations necessary to prepare China for the coming "utopia." Any idea that they're becoming a capitalist nation is at best naive, and at its worst, dangerous. Any steps toward the West is a well-planned act to save what is left of a smothered economy, while trying to build a new one, plus a cosmetic cover-up to hide the devastating bureaucratic bungling of an "elite" that according to Marxism is not even supposed to exist.

Just how firmly the Beijing leadership is in control is vividly portrayed in the present Anti-Crime Campaign.

In early August 1983, large numbers of criminal suspects were arrested. In a two-day period, August 6–8, 3,000 were arrested in Beijing, 5,000 in Shanghai and 6,000 in Tianjim. The total number of arrests during those first few days probably exceeded tens of thousands.

There were reports in Beijing that the local cadre leaders throughout China had been given quotas. They were ordered to produce a specific number of "criminals" in the same way that they were at other times to produce food, or other basic necessities of life. The difference this time is that a head count was easy and it was impossible to use the "rubber" yard stick used for other campaigns.

What this meant was that if you lived in an area where crime was low, that is, the people were law abiding, you could be arrested for a crime that you might have confessed, which was written under duress twenty years previous.

The fear that has struck the hearts of the people from this campaign is obvious when a foreigner attempts to make contact with the people on an informal basis. One tourist spent two days in Shanghai simply trying to make eye contact with Chinese citizens. Two years ago, you could not keep the crowds away; now it was just the opposite.

What is produced is a pyramid with the persons arrested being placed at different levels, peaking with the death penalty.

The Anti-Crime Campaign was officially ordered by the party at the Second Plenary Session of the Sixth National People's Congress which met in Beijing for nine days ending on September 2.

This congress authorized the new National Security Ministry (equal to the Soviet KGB) to take over the responsibility of investigating espionage suspects, plus passing a resolution implementing several punishments of criminal elements that "seriously harm the peace of the society." Included was the death penalty which until this time had been beyond the legal jurisdiction of local officials.

Consequently, those at the peak of the pyramid were and are still being executed. Who gets executed is dependent on the seriousness of the crimes of those at the lower level of the pyramid.

The first executions from the peak of the pyramid took place in Beijing on August 23, 1983, when 30 criminals were shot before an audience of 100,000 spectators who were bussed to the execution site. Many executions followed, including one observed by foreigners on a "private trip." They reported that the people were ordered to the streets to watch as trucks with machine guns mounted on the cabs paraded by. Between each of these trucks, which were also carrying soldiers of the People's

Liberation Army, was a truck with two prisoners. They stood in the front part of the truck facing the people, their hands were tied behind their backs. A rope was around their necks holding their head up. Two policemen held onto their shoulders. Their crimes were printed on banners and mounted above them. Of the forty trucks that were in the parade, twenty-two carried two prisoners each. These were "paraded" to a public park where they were made to kneel down, and a 45 calibre bullet ended their life.

Observers reported that "to stand with the people and feel the fear generated by such a parade was witness enough that these people meant business." It is all part of a saying in the streets: "Arrest some, jail some, kill some."

It is a campaign not only designated to attempt to control the realistic "crime-wave" that is sweeping China, but also an attempt to provide youthful laborers for development of the provinces which are underpopulated. These would be the provinces on the western and northwestern borders which are infamous for their devastating climatic conditions and almost unbearable living conditions. A Shanghai newspaper recently reported that "12,000 unemployed youths volunteered to help develop the country"—that is, "go west, young man," whether you want to or not.

Those who follow the tourist route report no unemployment, no crime, just a billion "happy, smiling people." They should listen to the conversation from a side street in any major city where "vacant buildings were being converted into temporary detention centers. Those arrested often have their urban residency permits confiscated (you need a permit to live in the cities) and then shipped off to remote provinces for labor reform."

Under Chinese law, a sentence of up to two years qualifies as an "administrative punishment" that requires no review.

In China's major cities police reportedly question youths loitering about public places and arrest anyone whose answer seems inadequate.

Another resident reports, far beyond the hearing of any tourist, who probably doesn't understand Chinese anyway, "Every night we hear the knocks, the arguments, the scuffles, and then sirens."

China is a tightly controlled totalitarian society, and every inch of freedom must be paid for by many yards of suffering. Control and suffering are not expected to change in the near future.

This "Anti-Crime Campaign" has been especially difficult for believers for several reasons. Some laws the believers cannot observe, such as abortion and infanticide. This places them in the category of "anti-revolutionary."

In places where there is a high ratio of Christians, there is an equally low ratio of crime. This means that Christians, innocent as they may be, will get caught in the quota system.

The official document announcing the campaign has a category #5, which covers "organizing reactionary groups" and "using feudalistic superstition to engage in anti-revolutionary activities." A house church meeting could be classified as an "organized reactionary group" and all Bible supply work, itinerant preachers and interpreters as not only anti-revolutionary, but "feudalistic superstition." This is the reason that "thirty house church leaders were arrested" at one time in Central China.

The facts of the situation are:

1. God's people and godly Christian leaders are being arrested or placed under severe pressure;
2. The party, in accordance with its religious policy formulated in March 1982, is cracking down on the house churches; and
3. The Three-Self/China Christian Council is the organ bringing pressure upon Christians to conform, despite skillfully mounted public relation exercises in China and abroad to convince the world that full religious liberty exists, and that they are the only "real" church in China.

The situation, although grave, is still not as bad as during the Cultural Revolution, when all religions were fiercely persecuted. At least people can attend the "open" churches and hear the gospel from some of the pastors. However, the situation is similar to that in the fifties when the Three-Self was used by the party to severely control the church. The big difference is that the church is both wiser and stronger spiritually, not to mention numerically, than it was then.

"Many Christians have passed through the trials of the fifties and sixties. Even if the harassment of the house churches should increase, with far more arrests, the church in China will survive and the gospel continue to spread. The modes of survival and propagation which the house churches have devised through experience over the last twenty years will stand them in good stead."

It is reasonable, then, to assume that China is and will continue to be a totalitarian state. Over a billion people held hostage by an elite few, who owe their continuous leadership to the machine of capitalism, including Christian tourists who spend several thousand dollars to invent new adjectives to describe only what the tourist guides want them to see.

Final Word on the TSPM

The *Three-Self Patriotic Movement* will continue to function. However, we shouldn't waste too much time on Bishop Ting, the present leader of the official clergy. He is dispensable and does only what he is told to do. The real power comes from Beijing, and that is why the TSPM will:

1. Continue to be a part of the official party structure, with one purpose: to identify and then to destroy the last vestige of "superstition," that is, Christianity in China. They will continue to retain the "official churches" for image purposes, but don't look for any program of evangelization.

2. Continue to be the official spokesman for the Protestant church in China. One has to remember how important image is to Beijing. Chou Enlai was about to receive the French Premier. All the Catholic churches were closed, most of the priests in prison. Chou had one of the churches reopened (it was a granary), the altar restored, a priest and some vestments dug up from a prison and a closet; they were ready for mass. The Premier decided not to attend mass, so the next day the boards went back up, the altar was torn down, the vestments disappeared along with the priest.

The TSPM will still attempt to woo Western Christian leaders, especially highly visible evangelical leaders to "come to China" and see how freedom of religion is a reality. Some may capitulate, reasoning that it is a chance to preach to Communist officials. The Chinese people would not know any of these "famous preachers." The show would be for those outside China, not those herded to the church for the TV cameras.

3. Continue to use all the power at their control to bring the house church under the official umbrella of the TSPM not only in word but in deed, that is, close all the house churches and send the pastors to "reeducation camps."

Radio: Telling "of God and His Love"

Radio, despite the fact that the TSPM has publicly announced that "Christian radio programs are hostile in character and believers should not listen," will continue to play a major role in the building of the church.

What would be hoped, however, is that there would be a new emphasis on Christian broadcasting directed to expositional Bible teaching.

There is a desperate need in the house church in China today for biblical teaching on matters of leadership, eldership, gifts of the Spirit, and the entire array of teachings that can come only from an understanding of God's Word.

There needs to be a greater realization that:

1. The best possible evangelistic message is expositional.
2. Good exposition, taking a book at a time, will cover, over a period of time, all of the needs in the body of believers, including arguments against Darwinism.
3. The job of Christian radio is not so much to compete with other organizations, such as Voice of America, Radio Moscow, etc., but rather to fulfill the unique mission of having a program content that none of the others will broadcast, that is, biblical preaching.

It is illegal to preach on the Second Coming of Christ from any pulpit (official or unofficial) in China. Radio has an opportunity seldom given, but hopefully never ignored.

Overseas Chinese: "Go . . ." into Your World

The future of the church in China can be greatly altered by overseas Chinese. For some time now, this group of people (with the exception of most in Hong Kong) have held many meetings—both large and small—on "How to Reach China," but in reality have done very little. Now, the overseas Chinese can make amends. They can give up their rather lofty positions in technical institutions, Christian denominations, seminaries and Bible schools, churches, and lose themselves in China as itinerant preacher/teachers.

As radio may be classified as the "electronic circuit-riding preacher" of this century, the overseas Chinese, with their training, language and ethnicity, can become the "in-resident circuit-riding preachers." Granted, there are considerable risks. The government does execute "spies," and that is what their classification may be. However, in this case, the opportunities seem to far surpass the risk.

They might take a lesson from two young men in China who had only a small amount of training in the Scriptures; however, they believed in the mission concept. They got themselves arrested in the Anti-Crime Campaign so that they could go as missionaries with those other "criminals" who were being sent to "rebuild the frontier." They felt the opportunity far exceeded the idea of a life of forced labor.

The Word

Concerning the printed page, the argument will continue as to the morality of "smuggling" Bibles and other literature into China. The TSPM will continue to vociferously denounce it, as will their like-minded brethren outside of China. The customs officers will continue to search people's luggage, and will confiscate whatever they find. The TSPM will continue to remind people that they can carry a couple of Bibles into China for friends and leave them at the official church, where they will either be stored or sold.

There will also be the promise by the TSPM to "print" a new

edition inside China, but the presses will probably never really start.

It would seem, at this point, to leave the entire question to the personal sensitive conscience of those who make requests for Bibles and to those who effectively make the "deliveries." It might still be appropriate for the rest of us to argue our case, as long as it does not interfere with the reality of the situation.

Real People: The People Problem

People problems will continue to plague the PRC (People's Republic of China). The official population of China is now 1 billion 29 million and growing by the hour. All of these people have to be fed, housed, educated and convinced not to procreate. In the future we can expect:

1. A much tougher birth control law which will increase mass abortion. This is especially difficult for believers, who, in China, like in other parts of the world, hold a fetus to be a living person, sacred in the eyes of God.
2. The one-child-per-family law will be more strictly enforced. Again this will be a special burden for the Christians in that they strongly oppose infanticide (especially killing baby girls) while at the same time desire to have a male child to carry on their tradition and take care of them in their old age.

China, which has the largest number of believers in the world, also seems to face the greatest number of seemingly insurmountable burdens with no relief promised for at least the foreseeable future.

Hong Kong: The Window, the Door, the Fire Escape

Hong Kong may be the most significant, or at least newsworthy, problem in China's future. It is a problem that had its genesis not in 1949, like so many of the others, but rather in 1842, when Great Britain acquired Hong Kong as a result of three treaties. In 1898, another treaty was signed which gave to Britain 350 square miles of adjoining territory known as "the New Territories."

The Hong Kong Island and the part of the New Territories known as Kowloon are at least that part where the big hotels have been built. Hong Kong Island and the New Territories were to be held by Great Britain for an undisclosed period of time, with the New Territories reverting to China on June 30, 1997.

Now China wants both the New Territories and Hong Kong/ Kowloon back. They don't want a divorce; they want an annulment. Beijing says that the treaties were made under duress, that is, gunpoint, and that this is one marriage that was never consummated.

As early as November of 1983, China gave Britain a "1984 deadline." Britain says they don't want to rush things, but China says they have already waited almost 100 years and now they want Hong Kong back.

Millions of dollars are already leaving the island each week, along with as many of the 5.5 million ethnic Chinese who can get visas to any country that will have them.

That activity points up the main reason that China cannot wait until 1997. If they did, there would be nothing left but empty vaults and high rise apartment buildings.

Basically, the majority of the Chinese living in Hong Kong either escaped from the Communist regime over the past forty years, or have relatives who have, but have now gone on to third countries. These people do not want to take the chance of living under the same regime that they escaped from. Nothing would stop Beijing from reeducating them one more time.

That "reeducation" would probably take place at various locations outside Hong Kong and would not include the entire family unit.

A large portion of the 5.5 million Chinese in Hong Kong are in this situation. They voted with their feet to leave China; they risked their lives to escape and now there is nowhere else to swim. They have reached the end of the line. They are candidates for another reeducation program on China's western frontiers.

Hong Kong is also significant for other reasons which must be considered.

1. It is the window to China. Those Christian Research Centers in Hong Kong that now keep the world informed as to the activity of the Three-Self Movement would not be welcomed as part of the new government. Consequently, the window to the church in China would not only be closed, but securely fastened shut. It is also the door into China.

2. Literature distribution in China is now almost entirely carried on from Hong Kong. This would cease.

3. Hong Kong now has a flourishing evangelical church; however, that would end.

4. Para-church activities, which serve not only China but other Asian countries as well, would cease to function.

Of this we can be sure, past insults must be corrected. China will take control of Hong Kong, and long before 1997. Many of the Chinese there will have to stay and face a future even more precarious than before they escaped from the Mainland. However, there will be no wide-spread persecution, at least not right away; that will come later. The take-over will be as gentlemanly as the British can allow the sun to set on that last empire; and the new Mandarins in the Mao jackets can prepare a dress rehearsal for a similar action in Taiwan.

In Summary

Though it is impossible to predict with any degree of accuracy on the future of the church in China—who could have or indeed did prophesy as to what has happened in the past decade—but it does seem that with a reasonable degree of accuracy we can suggest, if not predict, the following:

1. China will remain a tightly controlled totalitarian state.
2. There will be more Anti-Crime Campaigns as they are needed to bring people under tighter control and make that totalitarianism a reality.
3. The TSPM will continue to try to effectively control the house church.
4. The house church will keep growing.
5. Radio will continue to be a major source of teaching for the believers.

6. Bibles will continue to be delivered to the believers.
7. Overseas Chinese will be given the opportunity to be the kind of missionary not offered to every generation.
8. The people problem will continue, creating severe problems for Christians who will refuse to abide by the unwritten laws of abortion and infanticide, nor the written law of one child per family.
9. China will take over Hong Kong, gently, swiftly and with as little publicity as possible, as a dress rehearsal for a similar action in Taiwan.

Any one of these problems would be enough to drive a Westerner "over the wall," but China seems to have the resilience needed for survival. Maybe that is why the Lord has entrusted them with such great truths as we last saw lived out in the Book of Acts.

Chapter Eleven

Back Through the Turnstile

As one moves, ever so reluctantly, from a comfortable seat in the spectators' stands, back to an individual and personal life, there is the haunting desire to turn and take one last look back at the arena. In reality that is not necessary. After witnessing a re-creation of the Book of Acts, one doesn't need even a quick backward glance. Yet I am uncomfortably conscious of the fact that what I have seen and heard and then made a rather feeble attempt to record is cause for an excess of dissonance to well up inside me.

This encounter with the house church in China has not only exposed, but jabbed the raw nerve of my, if not comfortably smug, at least self-satisfied evangelical lifestyle.

The Book of Acts has always been exciting reading—as much a record of things past as the Book of Revelation is of things to come. Never did I suspect that in reality one crashed into the other.

But now, I have seen it happen. More than anything, I want to hurl myself into the arena, whatever the consequences. Then I realize I'm only a spectator.

That burning desire to be an actual participant is tempered by the realization that were I there, I would, in all probability, be one of those who didn't quite make it, one of the "if only's" of history.

Winding my way through the parking lot to my well-marked

territory of existence, with the glistening white lines that mark my parameters of belief, some thoughts begin to take form in my mind, thoughts tinged with a slight aura of jealousy, mingled with a heavy sadness.

While I was attending great world conferences on evangelism, here were a people evangelizing.

While I was signing covenants, statements of beliefs, with a ball point pen at some convention center, here were a people signing a covenant with their blood.

While I was reading one more book on how to be a "successful" Christian, here were people being inordinately successful.

While I was riding the crest of another wave of the future, here were a people plumbing the depths of present reality.

While I was listening with itching ears to arguments regarding the validity of signs, wonders and miracles, here were a people experiencing them.

While I was examining and arguing the validity of the manifestations of the gifts of the Spirit for this age, here were a people exercising them—all of them.

As I reach my car, unlock it, and move in behind the wheel, I have to lean my head back and rest for a moment. As I take a deep breath, the smell from the arena fills my nostrils. But there is something different. Filling my lungs, cleansing my mind, is a perfume that transcends the odor of blood, sweat, spoiled food and prison excrement.

My total being is transcended by a new song. The resonant notes of a cello are replaced by the quivering voice of an old man, "If I had a thousand hands, with a thousand fingers on each hand, I would gladly do it all over again."

I feel his gnarled, burn-scarred fingers reach over and gently touch my unmarred hands and again he speaks. "I once used these fingers to bring music from a mechanical instrument. But now I have Jesus Christ, and I *am* music."

Now it is my turn to shed a few tears. Before me I see a people who have so vividly illustrated the fact that when a person becomes a disciple of Jesus Christ, he does not think of it as some sanctified game of monopoly. There is no roll of the dice, the picking of a card, and the reading of the instructions: "Go directly to Pentecost, do not pass Gethsemane, do not stop at Calvary. Pick up your $100."

Here are a people who seem to understand, as perhaps I never will, that there are no shortcuts to Pentecost. To build the church is a battle that has to be won struggle by struggle—first the high ground, then the low ground.

Here are a people who seem to realize that this life is one long war, and in any war we must expect and accept casualties. There will be the wounded, there will be the suffering, there will be the dead. These people seem to understand in a way that makes my lips dry with desire that life is not a playground, but a battleground. They become Christians and enter the Bible college of life every day so that they may continue to go forth and turn the world upside down, instead of simply preparing to fit into an already comfortable society. They are willing to pay whatever tuition is imposed on them.

I can see the church of China walking, willingly, into the darkness of Gethsemane. Like Him, whom they serve so well, they could have simply said no, and who would have held them responsible for such an action. No one would have thought of them as quitters. After all they had been through, they certainly had the right to some of the comforts of being one of God's chosen people. They could have said: "No, I cannot stand one more betrayal from a brother or sister."

"No, I cannot take one more beating, one more day of humiliation, one more moment of mental anguish."

"No, I cannot say good-bye to one more loved one."

"No . . . no . . . no . . ."

But they didn't!

Later they would know why. They would see the contorted faces of those who had betrayed their Lord and fled naked into the obscure pages of Chinese history.

They knew that death in Gethsemane is not an option. Either you leave as a traitor, or stay and fight. They stayed, and they fought.

They certainly must have understood, in a way that I never will, what it is like to struggle in anguish while the rest of the believers sleep.

Surely, as they looked beyond the comfortable slumbering forms, silhouetted in the darkness, they could see the wine press—the instrument used to crush the stem, the skin, the seed, the flesh of the olive, so that one little drop of oil would slowly, painfully, and purposefully, fall into a waiting vessel.

Here were a people that said, "Let's go," and then made their way to Calvary. Gethsemane must have done for them what it has always done for those willing to pay that kind of price. They knew themselves to be sinful people. Never mind that others might have said, "No, you are wonderful," or, "No, you're not that bad." They knew just how bad they really were. They knew that they needed to have what they *were*, covered with the blood of the Lamb, so that they could come into the presence of the Lord so He could take care of what they *are*. Surely, they also realized that it was not enough to be delivered from what they *were*; they also needed the power to be what God wanted them to *be*. Slowly, surely, we can hear the quiet procession of the shuffling feet, from every part of China, as they made their way to a hillside; there was the sound of someone digging, and then, the "thump" of a cross being set upright; the pounding of nails, and slowly, old superstitions, ancestral worship, arrogance of being a superior race, bitterness for feeling they had been forgotten, ambitions, desires, security, creature comforts; the hills of China were alive with hundreds of years of history hanging from crosses. A twentieth-century Nero had helped purify Christ's church.

It was all there:

—The terrible handling by Mao's soldiers and Red Guards.

—The journey to the city square to be spat upon, to be unfairly sentenced, with the crowd shouting, "Punish them! Punish them!"

—The walks of shame through the villages, carrying the banner tied to their back with their crimes in bold letters for all to see and hiss at.

—The dunce caps on their heads, fitting like a crown of thorns. As they walked, surely they looked for a moment into the eyes of those who before had said, "I love you," and now shouted with the masses, "Kill them!"

—The beatings that continued all the way to the prison outside the city gates.

But then, something happened!

It is finished! What was finished? No more sorrow? No, that continues. No more pain? It is still there. But now for every crushing blow, there is applied the balm of Gilead. For every "why" there is "why not."

They speak as they had never spoken before. Their enemies are confused and frightened. Their words become arrows that pierce the hearts of their tormentors. Sick people become well. "Help" becomes "Hallelujah."

A chosen few from a distant land went to observe. They had difficulty understanding what they saw.

Soon they, too, began to realize that God truly does use the wrath of man to praise Him; that persecution is not destructive, but constructive; that He will, indeed, build His church and the gates of hell will not prevail against it. They saw a people who don't count casualties, but survivors.

The list could go on and on. One's heart burns with a desire to run back into the arena, but then there is the realization that turnstiles turn only one way. Perhaps someday, sometime, there will be another arena, and I will be there, but in the meantime here I am . . .

As one wipes his eyes, starts the car, and quietly heads for the freeway, and the reality of life, there are more tears, but this time they are not the scalding ones of fear, conviction, or repentance; rather, they are cool, comforting, the tears of praise and thanksgiving.

In the flow of traffic, the words come, slow and distinct: "Thank you, China, for being willing to pay the price."

Thank you to those who have already died, the unnumbered millions, buried in unmarked graves. To those still *faceless* and unremembered who even today continue to rot away in prisons. To those who are still being arrested at this hour; and to those who get themselves arrested so that they can be sent to slave labor camps as missionaries, thank you.

Thank you to that one who was willing to forget her twelve-year-sentence of cleaning the latrines while singing and praising the Lord, testifying, "It was wonderful! I had the cleanest latrines in the entire hospital."

Thank you to another member of the educated elite who shared a similar fate, and who would later testify, "As I scrubbed those latrines, I wept as I thought that this is what my Lord did for me. My heart was once like this latrine, but He died to wash it clean, and then I would scrub all the harder."

The list could go on and on. No matter how long I want to remember, the "thank you's" would continue.

Thank you for assuaging my frustrations with your tears of understanding; for mollifying my anger with your living testimonies; for massaging my aching heart with your broken fingers.

Thank you for sharing your secrets of survival.

Thank you for being real people, who shed real tears, so that I may taste one precious drop of the real salt of this earth.

Additional Information

If you would like to become more deeply involved with the church in China, or receive additional information, we suggest you contact the following:

Research on China and regular reports:

Dr. Jonathan Chao
CHINESE CHURCH RESEARCH CENTER
7 Kent Road, Flat A, Kowloon, Hong Kong

Direct involvement through literature and other materials:

Dr. Ted Shueh
CHRISTIAN COMMUNICATIONS, LTD.
P.O. Box 95364, Tsimshatsui
Kowloon, Hong Kong

Dr. David Wang
ASIAN OUTREACH
G.P.O. 3448
Hong Kong

OPEN DOORS WITH BROTHER ANDREW
P.O. Box 4282
Manila, Philippines

Sponsor or produce radio programs for China:

Mr. Ken Lo
Far East Broadcasting Associates
P.O. Box 9-6789, Tsimshatsui
Kowloon, Hong Kong

Mr. John Buerer
Trans World Radio
10th Floor, On Lee Bldg.
Kowloon, Hong Kong

Before you go to China, or even consider doing so, you should read two books:

China: Alive in the Bitter Sea by Fox Butterfield, Times Books, NY, 1982

Broken Earth: The Rural Class (in China), Free Press, NY, 1983

Other Marshall Pickering Paperbacks

THROUGH DAVID'S PSALMS

Derek Prince

Derek Prince, internationally known Bible teacher and scholar, draws on his understanding of the Hebrew language and culture, and a comprehensive knowledge of Scripture, to present 101 meditations from the Psalms. Each of these practical and enriching meditations is based on a specific passage and concludes with a faith response. They can be used either for personal meditation or for family devotions. They are intended for all those who want their lives enriched or who seek comfort and encouragement from the Scriptures.

LOVING GOD

Charles Colson

Loving God is the very purpose of the believer's life, the vocation for which he is made. However loving God is not easy and most people have given little real thought to what the greatest commandment really means.
Many books have been written on the individual subjects of repentence, Bible study, prayer, outreach, evangelism, holiness and other elements of the Christian life. In **Loving God,** Charles Colson draws all these elements together to look at the entire process of growing up as a Christian.
Combining vivid illustrations with straightforward exposition he shows how to live out the Christian faith in our daily lives. **Loving God** provides a real challenge to deeper commitment and points the way towards greater maturity.

OUT OF THE MELTING POT

Bob Gordon

Faith does not operate in a vacuum, it operates in human lives. God wants your life to be a crucible of faith.
Bob Gordon draws together Biblical principles and personal experience to provide valuable insights into this key area. Particular reference is made to the lessons he leant recently as God provided £600,000 to buy Roffey Place Christian Training Centre.
Out of the Melting Pot is Bob Gordon's powerful testimony to the work of God today and a profound challenge to shallow views of faith.

BILLY GRAHAM

John Pollock

By any reckoning, Billy Graham is one of the major religious figures of the twentieth-century.
John Pollock tells the highlights of the Billy Graham story briefly and vividly for the general reader. Using existing material and brand new information the story is taken right up the eve of Mission England.
This is an authoritative biography which pays special attention to the recent developments in Dr. Graham's life and ministry. Fully endorsed by Billy Graham himself, the book is full of fascinating new insights into the man and his mission.
". . . fascinating reading"

London Bible College Review

". . . a difficult book to put down"

Church of England Newspaper

THE TORN VEIL

Sister Gulshan and Thelma Sangster

Gulshan Fatima was brought up in a Muslim Sayed family according to the orthodox Islamic code of the Shias. Suffering from a crippling paralysis she travelled to England in search of medical help. Although unsuccessful in medical terms, this trip marked the beginning of a spiritual awakening that led ultimately to her conversion to Christianity.

Gulshan and her father also travelled to Mecca in the hope that God would heal her, but that trip too was of no avail. However, Gulshan was not detered. She relentlessly pursued God and He faithfully answered her prayers. Her conversion, when it came, was dramatic and brought with a miraculous healing.

The Torn Veil is Sister Gulshan's thrilling testimony to the power of God which can break through every barrier.

NOW I CALL HIM BROTHER

Alec Smith

Alec Smith, son of Ian Smith the rebel Prime Minister of Rhodesia whose Unilateral Declaration of Independence plunged his country into twelve years of bloody racial war, has written his own story of those years.

The story of his life takes him from early years of rebellion against his role as 'Ian Smith's son' through his youth as a drop-out, hippy and drug peddler into the Rhodesian forces.

A dramatic Christian conversion experience at the height of the civil war transformed his life and led to the passionate conviction to see reconciliation and peace in a deeply divided country.

What follows is a thrilling account of how God can take a dedicated life and help to change the course of history.

HOW TO MANAGE PRESSURE
Before Pressure Manages You

Tim LaHaye

Pressure is unavoidable. Everyone faces pressure in some area of their life. Even as you read this, you may be aware of pressures in your life that cause worry and tension and hinder your sense of well being.
The good news of this book is that there is a way to handle pressure so that it can become a creative rather than destructive force.
Tim LaHaye offers insights that will enable you to relieve stress and to live a more satisfying life amidst those everyday pressures.

LOVE LIFE FOR EVERY MARRIED COUPLE

Dr E. Wheat

Dr Wheat, a physician and therapist, has helped thousands of troubled couples improve their love lives and build happier marriages with his unique counselling methods. In **Love Life for Every Married Couple**, Dr Wheat explores marital conflict in a straightforward manner, focusing on the reasons why couples experience frustration and unhappiness in their love lives.

"Dr Wheat has revealed, again, his unique talent for identifying the critical issues in family living, and then offering wise counsel and loving support to those who hurt . . . I recommend Love Life to those who want a better marriage." Dr James Dobson

RELEASE
The Miracle of the Siberian Seven

Timothy Chmykhalov with Danny Smith

The plight of the 'Siberian Seven' attracted widespread publicity and support.
Timothy Chmykhalov, youngest member of the seven, vividly recounts the events leading to the entry into the US Embassy in 1978, the long years of hoping and waiting, the uncertainty which faced them when they left in 1983 and finally the freedom which they found in America.
Release is a powerful testimony of faith and courage amidst intense pressure and threat of persecution. A story of hope and determination in the face of much discouragement.

SURVIVOR

Tania Kauppila

Born into poverty, forced to endure filth and slave labour in a Nazi concentration camp, how did Tania Kauppila survive? When Nazi occupation forces arbitrarily decreed that one member from each family in the Russian city of Rovno must "serve the war effort" for a "three month" period in Germany, 12 year old Tania insisted that she be the one to go from her family. She was young and strong and her father was needed by her sick mother and younger brother.
At age 12, Tania had already experienced incredible hardships and had seen more of life's harsh realities than most women ever see. When she left her family – the only security she knew – she faced frightening, unanswerable questions. How would she survive? Would she ever see her family again? Would she ever find the God of her father? Would she ever find peace?
Survivor is the story of an incredible life spanning three continents and five decades. It is a witness to the sustaining strength and love of a God who will not let go.